Eddy Brimson was born in Hemel Hempstead, in 1964, and after leaving school, he trained as a graphic designer. He is married to Harriet, a Gooner!

He is co-author, with his brother Dougie Brimson, of four previous books, *Everywhere We Go*, *England, My England*, *Capital Punishment* and *Derby Days* – all of which were published by Headline. On his own he has written a novel, *Hooligan*, and presented and narrated a video of his World Cup experiences called *Teargas and Tantrums*.

Also by Eddy Brimson and Dougie Brimson

Everywhere We Go
England, My England
Capital Punishment
Derby Days

Also by Eddy Brimson

Hooligan

Tear Gas and Ticket Touts

With the England Fans at the World Cup

Eddy Brimson

HEADLINE

First published in 1999
by HEADLINE BOOK PUBLISHING

10 9 8 7 6 5 4 3 2 1

ISBN 0 7472 6208 X

Typeset by Avon Dataset Ltd, Bidford-on-Avon, Warks

Printed and bound in Great Britain by
Mackays of Chatham plc, Chatham, Kent

HEADLINE BOOK PUBLISHING
A division of Hodder Headline PLC
338 Euston Road
London NW1 3BH

Dedication

This book is dedicated to football fans everywhere, especially Wiltshire, Mr B., Gary, Tony, Pete F., A. L. and all those that actually travelled to France '98. Many thanks also go to Ian Marshall at Headline, but as ever my greatest appreciation goes to my wife Harriet, the most understanding and wonderful football widow on the planet. Thank you for your support 'H-Bomb', I love you millions.

Teargas and Tantrums, a video diary of France '98, is also available via Carlton Home Entertainments.

Contents

Introduction *Who's a Naughty Boy Then?*   1

Diary

1 *Ready for the Big Kick-off*
  Day 1: Wednesday, 10 June 1998   5

2 *Viva Chile*
  Day 2: Thursday, 11 June   15

3 *Boring*
  Day 3: Friday, 12 June   19

4 *Out of Africa*
  Day 4: Saturday, 13 June   21

5 *'Ere we go, 'Ere we go, 'Ere we go . . . Oh no!*
  Day 5: Sunday, 14 June   25

6 *Life's A Beach*
  Day 6: Monday, 15 June   55

7 *Oh, I Do Like to be Beside the Seaside!*
  Day 7: Tuesday, 16 June   85

8 *Calm Down, Calm Down: For God's Sake, Calm Down*
  Day 8: Wednesday, 17 June   101

9 *Touts and Tensions Rising*
  Day 9: Thursday, 18 June   109

10 *Fuck Football, Let's Dance*
   Day 10: Friday, 19 June   119

11 *Tonight is Quiz Night*
   Day 11: Saturday, 20 June   127

12 *And So To War*
   Day 12: Sunday, 21 June   133

13 *Living Out The Dream – Well, Almost*
   Day 13: Monday, 22 June   145

14 *Hello The Wife, Bye Bye The Jocks*
   Day 14: Tuesday, 23 June   157

15 *Penalty, Ref! Oh, All Right Then*
   Day 15: Wednesday, 24 June   163

16 *USA, Nil Points*
   Day 16: Thursday, 25 June   165

17 *Lens Or Bust*
   Day 17: Friday, 26 June   167

18 *Tired*
   Day 18: Saturday, 27 June   189

19 *The Boring Art of Making History*
   Day 19: Sunday, 28 June   193

20 *Just Popping Out Again, Love*
   Day 20: Monday, 29 June   195

21 *Serious Argy-Bargy*
   Day 21: Tuesday, 30 June   199

22 *Whatever Happened To 'The Breat British Press'?*   225
23 *What Way Next For Football's Finest?*   229
24 *Is That It Then?*   245

Introduction
Who's A Naughty Boy Then?

Every Saturday from August through to May I pay my money and bow to the religion that is football and, as a supporter of live football, France '98 was just too good an opportunity to be missed no matter what the advertising campaigns said in order to discourage me. I believed that the World Cup finals tournament would provide an entirely different experience from the addiction I crave for week in week out and so as soon as the England team booked their ticket, so did yours truly.

Like so many devotees to the faith I just can't break free from the habit of travelling to the likes of Carlisle, Sunderland and Plymouth for Tuesday night matches in support of my club, and yes, I can honestly say with my hand on my heart that many of those long midweek away trips have turned out to be wet, cold and windy. Yet I wouldn't have missed any of them for the world because every one of those trips has provided me with a lasting memory. Carlisle – my first away trip on a football special. Plymouth – a 1–0 win that sent Watford FC top of the table. And Sunderland – a night when 800 Hornets outsung 30,000 Makems in the Stadium of Light, despite a 4–1 defeat. It's only when watching football live that such memories manifest, and when I say 'live' I don't mean 'Live on Sky'.

1

I am not a fan of TV football; you never get the whole event. You miss the banter, the smell. When the sport becomes a television show it's over and done with in just 90 clinical minutes. In armchair land football is always warm, comfortable and safe, missing that one magical ingredient: atmosphere. Yet in the raw football has everything and it is everything that I love. I love to sit among like-minded people (although given the choice I would rather stand), singing my heart out in support of the lads who proudly pull on the colours of my club or country. I adore the special atmosphere that only live football can provide.

Of course, by not being a member of 'The Official England Members Club', I was advised to pass on this once-in-a-lifetime opportunity, told to stay at home while France rocked. I was a naughty little boy, undeserving because I hadn't paid my £17 membership fee. But my dreams are not that easily broken, and as I have never had a liking for anything 'official' I decided to bunk off and head south anyway. Sad to think that even as a sorry old thirty-something, that childhood trait of rebelling against whatever you're told not to do still has a firm grip on me; and I guess that must go for the other 20,000 that 'unofficially' made the trip as well.

I travelled to France for many reasons. I went in support of my country, not ashamed to say that I am English and proud in a time when such statements are oh so politically incorrect. I had a dream of being able to say 'I was there; I experienced the World Cup finals' and I had a burning desire to prove to myself and those money-grabbing bastards who continually ruin the great game that no matter how hard they make it I, along with thousands of other fans, will always find a way in which to continue the love affair we all hold with the game.

As I hadn't travelled away with the England fans for over ten years I also wanted to witness first hand whether or not the game had indeed taken the great leap forward we keep hearing so much about, although the build-up to the tournament, the allocation of tickets and the general disorganisation hadn't exactly crammed my head full of confidence. However, the one thing I knew France '98 could provide was a unique opportunity to live among true football supporters from all over the globe for a whole glorious month of footy-related heaven.

In truth I left England not quite knowing what to expect, my head full with a mixture of hope, excitement and fear. I had no match tickets, no hotels booked and just myself for company, but I was soon to discover that when following the England team abroad you are never alone; we were all English, all in it together. Within these pages I have done my best to describe the highs and lows of what proved to be an unforgettable trip. In many ways France '98 was also a test, a test of my faith in this great game and the fans who are, and will always remain, its lifeblood. I wanted to prove that I wouldn't be beaten by men who only see this form of religion as a money-making machine.

I have in no way tried to smooth around the edges and at times I may appear to contradict myself, but the feelings I express during certain events were very real at the time and so I have laid them out in an honest and true account of what I witnessed first hand; something that could well cost me a few of the friends I made along the way.

Teargas and Ticket Touts is just one man's account of France '98, the story of an average football fan who wanted to be there, took a chance and came up trumps. This book poses numerous questions as to the treatment handed out to football supporters left to fend for themselves on foreign soil, but in no way have I tried to offer any answers to the problems that so many had to endure.

I headed off in search of a new football supporting experience, and believe me, being an English fan in France during the summer of '98 was one hell of an experience.

I hope you enjoy it. I know I did.

Ready for the Big Kick-off
Day 1: Wednesday, 10 June 1998

At last the opening day has arrived, and France '98 is about to get underway. I must admit that all the pre-tournament hype has already left me with a feeling of football overkill. I can't help thinking to myself as I open my 'World Cup official brand' cornflakes that the sooner Scotland get beaten, by Brazil this afternoon and restore some much-needed reality to this football-crazy world the better.

I switch on the television just in time for some breakfast newscaster to inform me that, while out in Paris the previous evening, the footballer and livewire of the dressing room Stan Collymore has had a run-in with his girlfriend, Ulrika Jonsson. Despite being dropped from the England squad, Stan still turns up in France and then, rather unwisely, thinks that despite being an England international he should pay a visit to a bar full of drunken Scotsmen. Finally, to cap it all, he then ends up in a bust-up with the Swedish beauty after unsuccessfully trying to persuade her to leave the premises with him. Amazing!

The next item brings more bad news as pictures of fans clashing with riot police flick across the screen. The reporter relays the news that these are local French hooligans fighting with Moroccans and Tunisians. All the groups were out to score points off each other, and it is reported that at one stage over

150 youths were involved in running battles with the police, who were forced to use teargas. These must be the local hooligans the media have been telling Joe Public never existed; the French supposedly didn't have a hooligan problem! Personally, the pictures don't come as much of a surprise, and the 'France '98 nick-o-meter' clicks into action early following over 30 arrests in Paris, of which only two were reported to be Scots. It is also reported in one of the broadsheets that over 100 known Scottish hooligans have already arrived in France and are being tracked by the security forces. Apparently the authorities' main concern is that they might join up with English hooligans in order to form a 'super firm' and cause major problems, a statement that proves once again that the police haven't got a clue.

And so it's off to watch the opening game. Now for an Englishman the only place to be is anywhere but a bar full of Jocks, and so to start the tournament off I've decided to sample the kind of environment the corporate punters enjoy so much. I soon find myself five pounds lighter and in the 'Club Lounge' at the home of football that is Vicarage Road, Watford.

Now let me state at this stage that I am not a Jock hater. OK, so I do think there has to be something strange about a race of people that seem to think ginger hair is something to celebrate, but we English have Morris dancers so that kind of evens things up. For the record, I have many friends north of the border as I once lived on one of the west coast islands and had a great time; however, when it comes to football, life takes on a different edge for most of us, and I am no exception.

To illustrate this point, I would like to share with you a letter I received through my P.O. box in the build-up to this tournament. I think Paul of Inverness states quite eloquently his feelings towards his English cousins:

Dear Prick,
I am writing just to let you know that I think all English football fans are the scum of the world. You think nothing of battering and trashing innocent people and should

therefore all be shot at birth. If I had my way I would starve all you English bastards. I come from the Highlands of Scotland and I am not worried one bit by your so-called hooligans. I have travelled to Wembley on many occasions and given some English scum the hiding they all deserve. They were good times, taking over London and kicking arse. You will never get the better of Scotland you fucking English pigs. Remember 1977? We really kicked the shit out of you that day. While we are talking about it, can't you sing anything other than Ingger-land? You poofy English pigs. Would you ever come to Scotland? Would you bollocks. Scotland the brave, England the cowards. I hate you fucking hypocrites. If all you can write about is violence then you should be ashamed of yourself you two-faced English wanker. Do you know that the English are the most hated people in the world? I hate you. I am Scottish and proud of it. We are good, good people unlike you English bastards. Braveheart rules OK! You wanker, eat my shit.

Now I think there may just be a hidden message in Paul's letter, but what he fails to understand is that for my mother's sins I am an Englishman, and therefore I couldn't give a fuck what he thinks.

By kick-off time the room is only a quarter full and Luther Blissett is the star attraction, while diligently playing host. Luther Blissett, top man. On the big screen we are flashed images from the carnival that is France '98, but for some outside the Stade de France, as Matty from Stirling quickly found out, the carnival had already turned into a nightmare:

As you would expect, the place was packed with people desperate for tickets. The atmosphere was fantastic with all the fans mixing in well, dancing and singing and just taking it all in. All over the place were the local kids, real arrogant little shits they were. They were really starting to piss people off, pushing and bumping into people.

There were all sorts of rumours flying around about them pick-pocketing people's tickets, and there was talk of someone being stabbed. My girlfriend was really starting to get annoyed when all of a sudden a fight broke out right next to us.

This little kid, no more than about ten, had tried to pull this guy's sporran from his kilt and so the guy had kicked him up the arse and told him where to get off. Within seconds there were about thirty of these little bastards all jostling around and shouting, some with small sticks in their hands. Then they started throwing stones and bottles, and as people began to run out of the way my girlfriend got knocked to the floor. As I went to pick her up some little bastards ran out and smacked me across the back. A few of the Scottish lads started to have a go back, but this lot just legged it. Then a couple of coppers turned up and started having a go at us lot. When some Scottish bloke had a go at them for doing fuck all, one of the coppers raised his baton and threatened to club him. Fucking idiots.

All in all 25 French youths were arrested in the stadium area before the game even kicked off. It was also reported that in the centre of Paris one fan had been repeatedly stabbed, and that a Scottish supporter had been found unconscious up an alleyway by a local taxi driver, and was taken to a police station. Once the supporter had been questioned he filed a report stating that he had been approached by two men trying to sell him drugs. When he had refused their offer, one of the drug pushers had attacked him and then he had been sexually assaulted by the other. Perhaps next time he'll leave his kilt in the wardrobe.

The occasion had also gone tits up for over 2,000 Brazilians who had journeyed halfway around the world only to find that the Spanish agency they paid £3,000 for match tickets failed to come up with the goods. Why do I have a feeling this won't be the last time this story is told during this tournament?

One other person who very nearly missed the match was that famous Scottish nationalist Sean Connery. Sean found himself shaken and stirred by security guards who escorted him away from the tunnel when he went to wish the Scottish team good luck.

Back in the safety of the 'Club Lounge' I've been joined at my table by one of the suits, his wife and her mum. Marvellous! As the greatest sporting event in the world kicks off my excitement is shattered as the suit's wife turns to Old Mother Hubbard and informs her that her sister Judy has just bought a seven-month-old Beagle puppy and that she really must go and see it. Simultaneously, on the table next to us another suit struggles to find his mobile phone as it goes off for the first of what turns out to be many times. Desperately, I try to focus in on the screen and blank out the world I've landed myself in.

Thankfully, Brazil score. 'Yesssss!' As I rise from my seat and punch the air I quickly realise that I am the only Brazilian fan in the room. Half-cocked, I look around. What is wrong with these people? Surely they can't all want the sweaties to win? It's time to pick up my pint and move away to the back of the room, a social outcast.

As the game continues I desperately want to cheer as the Scottish number 10 Darren Jackson provides the cameraman with our first visible 'fuck off' of the tournament, but I restrain myself and continue eating my complimentary chips in a basket alone. Suddenly, the silence is broken. At first it looks as if the referee has given the Scots a penalty; surely not. A half-baked cheer hits the air. Then the realisation hits me: the ref *has* given a penalty. I want to scream at the screen, 'REF, YOU ARE FUCKING JOKING', but somehow I feel that, as before, it would be best if I kept my mouth shut. Scotland score and five or six blokes jump up. They are joined by three or four others who appear as if they really want to join in but don't quite know why. I can't help thinking that this has to be some kind of nightmare from which I shall wake up at any moment.

At half-time I suddenly find myself under pressure as Old

Mother Hubbard comes heading my way.

'I hope we didn't drive you away from your table.'

'No,' I lie. 'Of course not, don't worry.'

She then starts to quiz me on how I think England will do before moving on to tell me why she feels that Sheringham should have been dropped as well as Gascoigne. This is followed by a heartfelt rant against Glenn Hoddle backed up by an equally intense defence of the Watford manager, Graham Taylor. Suddenly I become a little scared as this old lady knows way too much and I am about to find myself out of my depth. Thankfully, I am rescued by the arrival of her complimentary chicken drumsticks. As a vegan, I never before thought I'd be thankful for Bernard Matthews, but on this occasion I'll give the mass animal murderer the benefit of the doubt as I'm sure he's going to hell anyway.

As the second half progresses I am becoming more uneasy. For some reason I get the feeling that Scotland might just do the unthinkable. Already they have had a dodgy penalty, and Jim Leighton is having a blinder. Brazil just don't seem to be getting the bounce of the ball either. I try to console myself with the fact that they will probably cock it up against Morocco anyway, and then the heavens open, God does his stuff and Boyd scores a glorious own goal. Once again I find myself on a desert island of joy as the rest of the room falls quiet. Oh thank you, Lord. Thank you for Scotland and slapstick football.

The final whistle goes and I am out of the door quicker than an FA panel can dismiss a Conference club's ground grading application. The drive home only adds to the warm feeling of joy as I listen to Nicky Campbell on Radio 5. Poor Nicky is one very disappointed Scotsman, consoling himself with support from other disappointed Scotsmen. I love football at times like this.

Meanwhile, up in Glasgow, Jason has spent the afternoon standing in a mudbath getting soaked to the skin with a few thousand pals:

While the rest of the world focuses in on a small patch of

green in the middle of sunny Paris, four thousand-odd idiots have made their way through the wind and rain so that they can stand shoulder to shoulder knee-deep in mud. It could only happen in Scotland. It may well be pissing with rain, but the macs and umbrellas remain the property of girlies, children and the odd Englishman trying to go unnoticed at the back. Give me a T-shirt, kilt, nylon wig and a reminder that the rain can only get you so wet, and we're away. 'Flower of Scotland' and free-flowing lager, I wouldn't miss this for the world, as this could be the moment Scotland comes of age.

The camera passes by the Brazilian team and suddenly the realization hits home that we are playing the greatest team on earth. Please lads, don't get slaughtered, no more humiliation please. A draw would be heavenly.

The game starts, Brazil score and the drizzle bites home. The goal, mixed with the lukewarm lager, brings sobering reality. Why am I putting myself through this? I feel like a contestant in the wet T-shirt competition from hell. Some are too pissed to care and continue to sing their heads off. Ah, what the fuck, we were never going to win the bloody thing anyway.

The game continues and our lads never get the break. Then the shout goes up and I can't but help join the throng, 'PENALTY, YA BASTARD!' The injustice of it all: they'd have been given a penalty for sure. The crowd around me goes mad as pictures of the Scottish players congratulating themselves fill the screen. My God, it is a penalty! My mind keeps telling me no, no, it can't be. This is Scotland. Scotland don't get penalties. My body goes ape before regaining composure. I am now still, calm, hands on cheeks, waiting, waiting. Collins steps up and shatters the aura of inner peace that I display to my companions. 'YEEESSSS! GO ON YA BASTAAAAAAARD!' Six long minutes pass by, then half-time. The dancing, singing and air of disbelief continue.

11

The game restarts. Leighton is playing out of his skin, the Brazilians look like St Mirren on a bad day and Scotland string passes together. The crowd falls quieter. It's a sign, a sign that we may just be standing on the edge of greatness. I have no nails left, so I start on my wig. I don't want the ref to blow his whistle. This time we can win, we really can. Brazil are rubbish, past it, nothing.

Enter the slippery fruit. Leighton saves once more. It's a good save. If it were Seaman it would be a great save. The ball bounces away from danger to find Tommy Boyd, who just happens to be passing through on his way to the comedy hall of fame. Slowly, slowly, the ball slips back past our saviour Jim and the dream dies. Even the Brazilian players appear to take the piss as they reel away laughing. Somehow you just knew that was going to happen.

'COME ON SCOTLAND. WE CAN DO THIS!' The words ring out around me, and the feeling with which they are shouted is real. Now the minutes flash by. We have our chances, but time catches up and it's over. The disappointment is as cold as the Glasgow rain. Four thousand rain-soaked Scotsmen, women and children applaud their heroes from the pitch, truly disappointed at only losing by the odd goal to the greatest team in the world. My friends and I console ourselves with the fact that we really are disappointed at losing. There is a saying that every dog has its day. Unfortunately I, like most other Scottish people, appear to be a cat person.

A Scottish friend of mine, Ally, actually managed to get into the game. For him, the occasion felt slightly different:

To tell the truth, it all seemed an anti-climax. Months of anticipation, the planning, then suddenly it's all over just like that. It was disappointing to see so many fellow Scotsmen left outside, heart-breaking. Some actually crying at the thought of missing out on what was meant to be our greatest moment. Then you get in the stadium only to see fans from all the different countries, and that rams it home. Football isn't for the likes of us any more, not for the likes of those left outside anyway. I was proud of the team. The players were magnificent, every one of them, but I would have loved to have been able to share it with more of my own, while belting out 'Flower of Scotland' for all the world to hear.

I spend the night watching Morocco and Norway run each other ragged from the safety of my own front room, and can't help thinking that Scotland might as well pack it in already to save themselves from any further embarrassment. As I settle myself down, my delight at Scotland's defeat is given an extra boost as the scorer of the own goal, Tommy Boyd, is quoted as saying, 'It's hard to explain how bad it feels.' Oh go on, Tommy, try, please try, just for me.

The Moroccan Hadji scores an unbelievable goal to put the Africans in front, but this is soon followed by the kind of own goal you would expect from the worst defender, playing for the worst team, in the worst Sunday morning league you could possibly find on the Outer Hebrides. The fantastically named Chippo is the Moroccan defender to provide such amusement. Morocco take the lead again, only for the player with a name best used to describe a contender for the arse Olympics gold medal, Eggen, to equalise. Final score 2–2.

Viva Chile

Day 2: Thursday, 11 June

On breakfast television they show a representative from the British consulate in Marseille stating that there are plenty of tickets flying around on the black market and that even they are receiving calls every day offering more. An interview is then shown with an English bar owner who informs the world that you can get tickets for any England game if you're prepared to pay £150. Yee ha! Roll on Monday.

Today I have conned the wife into thinking we are off to London for a pre-holiday shopping trip. At 4.15 p.m. we find ourselves sitting in La Tavernetta, an Italian restaurant in the heart of Soho. With 15 minutes to go before the kick-off of Italy v. Chile I ask the waiter for his prediction. 'Italy has no chance,' he pronounces. 'They have no one to score the goals; Baggio is an old man who can only score against the poor teams. Salas [the Chilean striker] will rip them apart.' When I try to stamp my own knowledge on the conversation by informing him that Chile haven't won a World Cup finals fixture since 1950, he just shrugs his shoulders and tells me that he is Romanian and couldn't really give a toss. On further questioning I find that the other waiter is Yugoslavian and that the cook is American. Suddenly I feel a little cheated by my surroundings.

All of us look on in admiration as we watch the Chilean

team belt out their national anthem. Did they mean that or what? Instantly, I am converted and swear my support for the South Americans.

The game starts and Italy take the lead. Silence from the kitchen. Approaching half-time and Salas equalises; the cries from the back room have the wife spitting pasta in my general direction. All this is costing me about 50 quid; where's the Italian passion I wanted to experience?

My wife, having taken a keen interest in the game, suddenly turns to me. 'Just think, the whole of Chile will be going mad now!'

What a great image that conjures up. I hold that thought for a moment. If the people of Chile share the same passion and belief as their players showed during the playing of their national anthem, then surely at this very moment that goal will have them invading Peru, about to turn their attention on the Argies.

We leave at half-time and make our way to Bar Italia around the corner. The atmosphere couldn't be more of a contrast. The bar is packed solid with exiled Italian stallions and girls on the pull. Despite the drizzle, more stand on bread crates outside in order to gain a glimpse of the big screen. The passion they display is just as you would expect from full-blooded Italians, arms shooting skywards whenever danger threatens. When Salas puts the Chileans 2–1 ahead the scene becomes more like that of a Mafia funeral: heads in hands, arms flying around, wailing cries and shouting. I could have murdered a coffee, but could I get one? Could I bollocks. For 40 minutes me and the wife are gasping until finally Baggio scores, the place goes mental and normal service is restored.

I arrive home just in time to watch Cameroon and Austria draw 1–1. The game is dreadful, and as always David Pleat is talking shite. However, he does provide the only moment of any note when he shares with us his opinion of the Austrian striker, Toni Polster, whom he believes has been totally ineffective. Two minutes later Mr Toni scores the equaliser, begging the question why, oh why, oh why does the box insist on inflicting him on us?

As the Cameroon team console themselves with only a point, off the pitch Marc-Vivien Foe, left out of the Cameroon squad due to a broken leg, describes the treatment he hopes to receive: 'The healers have said they will be able to cure me in three days by burying my leg in the ground and putting fire around it. They have also recommended massage with gorilla bones while invoking the spirits of ancestors.' And they complain in England about Eileen Drewery.

Boring
Day 3: Friday, 12 June

The day starts with more hysterical news items concerning the black market for tickets that is sweeping France. English and Scottish fans are not alone in getting ripped off as hundreds of Japanese have arrived in France only to find that, just like the Brazilians, their tickets never existed. Masami Tachi, a Tokyo housewife on the trip of a lifetime, did, however, have a few comforting words for their tour rep: 'We're going to take our tour co-ordinator hostage, but we will not kill him.' Just like the Kray twins, those Japs – hard but fair.

More worrying for me personally is the news that a group of over 200 Argentinian Nazis are reported to be heading for Marseille in order to fight any Englishmen they can find. Bastards. I wouldn't have backed their team to win the bloody thing if I'd have known. The news has the wife worried. I try to pass it off but she is not convinced: inside, neither am I. News also comes through regarding the first Scottish hooligan arrested during the violence that took place the night before the tournament started. Despite admitting he threw bottles at the local police, Christopher Kyle only receives a two-month suspended sentence. The judgement allows him to continue following Scotland as he walks free from a Paris courtroom – not the stiff warning the Home Secretary would have liked the French to send out on the day before most English fans start travelling.

In the afternoon Bulgaria draw 0–0 with Paraguay in what turns out to be a terrible game.

Bobby Robson, the ex-England manager, blinds us with his powers of observation as he points out that a European side has yet to win a match in France '98. Wow, wise words indeed considering only one of the matches played so far has failed to end in a draw. Within three hours the Danish have shattered King Bobby's words of wisdom following a less than convincing 1–0 win over Saudi Arabia.

And so we come to the opening match for the host nation, France, the only sensible place to watch the game being the pub. Before kick-off I talk to a friend of mine who moans about all these 'new' football fans filling up his pub. He then informs me that he loved the Cameroon v. Austria match: 'It was like watching sackcloth against silk.' I stare back in silence. What a dick!

I see the first goal, hear the booing directed at the black South African players from the home fans, but miss the rest of the game due to boredom: when is the tournament actually going to get exciting? France go on to win 3–0.

Out of Africa
Day 4: Saturday, 13 June

Today starts on yet another low note as more scare stories about rampaging Argentinian Nazis fill column inches for the newspaper editors. The story goes that the Barra Brava (that's 'wild bunch' to me and you) are now teaming up with a gang of French Nazis and heading England's way. Apparently they have killed 37 people in the last eight years and over 1,500 supporters have been stabbed during organised violence. It is also rumoured that they have seventies-style haircuts and don't like their mums very much.

For me personally the competition so far has been a bit of an anti-climax, but today all that changes as the Nigerian team takes the field for the first time. Their opponents, Spain, have enjoyed a fantastic build-up to the tournament, but the Africans soon stamp their own claim on the trophy. Despite trailing the Spanish twice, the Nigerians never once lose their composure or self-belief, and at times remind me of the Brazilians at their best. One of the highlights of the game is the major bollock dropped by Zubizarreta, the Spanish goalkeeper, as he spoons Lawal's low shot into his goal. Other people's disasters are so sweet to watch, yet even that glorious moment is eclipsed by the winning strike by Oliseh from fully 25 yards. For the first time during France '98 I jump from my seat with excitement, and I still have the cat's claw marks to prove it!

The low point of the game came just before Oliseh's strike when a Nigerian player went to take the throw-in leading to the goal. The ball had gone off the pitch down by the corner flag, just in front of a large group of Spanish fans. As the Nigerian player picked up the ball you could clearly hear some Spanish fans making ape noises, as had the French supporters during their game. For me that made the winning goal all the more sweet. Sweeter still was the fact that the Nigerians held their goal celebrations down in that very same corner.

The next game up is Mexico v. South Korea. Now I know it's cheap, but I have to say it. The names of the South Korean squad read like the menu from a Thai restaurant – Min-Sung, Do-Hoon, Jong-Soo – every one a winner, and I couldn't help but begin to feel a bit peckish. Then I catch the name of the manager: Cha Bum-Kun. Suddenly I'm not quite so hungry.

The game itself has everything. Once again we start with a shock when Ha Seok-Ju (bean curd in black bean sauce) puts the Asians ahead, giving us the chance of another major upset. This is what the World Cup is all about. Then we have an unbelievable piece of skill from the Mexican number 11 Blanco who, when approached by two defenders, grips the ball between his two feet and bunny hops between them in order to get clear – fantastic. It took me back to when Johann Cruyff fooled not only the defender in front of him, but the whole world back in 1974 when this same competition was held in what was then known as West Germany. What Cruyff did that day was to me the greatest moment in football I have ever seen, and the next day every kid at school was trying to repeat the feat.

The second half is fascinating as Mexico power forward. Pelaez equalises, but the South Koreans do all they can to hold out before two late strikes by Hernandez clinch all three points for Mexico.

The day's football is finished off by what is without doubt the most boring game of the tournament so far: Holland 0, Belgium 0. I watch the match in a pub where the people around me delight in constantly mentioning the fact that Marseille is one of the most dodgy places to visit in Europe. The thought that by this time tomorrow night I shall be in that very city, on my own and with nowhere to stay is starting to have the old bum twitching.

On the final news item of the day it is reported that the Football Association are so worried about possible crowd trouble that they have sent out their own representative to help the local police stop England fans buying tickets on the black market. With 20,000 Englishmen expected in the city over the coming days, I can't help thinking that the FA are going to have their work cut out. The excitement mixed with the worry makes getting to sleep virtually impossible.

'Ere we go, 'Ere we go,
'Ere we go . . . Oh no!

Day 5: Sunday, 14 June

The first day of my trip to France '98 starts badly. I spend 30 minutes on the train station platform trying to convince my wife that I'll be OK. Finally the moment comes when the minute hand clicks around, indicating that the train is late. 'Bollocks!' Fifteen more minutes, followed by another 15 minutes. 'Where's the fucking train?' I panic, and resort to begging the wife to drive me to Waterloo station.

The Eurostar terminal is buzzing with England fans and Old Bill. I soon find out that most of the supporters are in the same boat as me: no tickets and nowhere to stay. That makes me feel a little bit better about the situation. During one conversation I have with two Spurs fans a lad comes over and asks if we're looking for match tickets. He is well spoken and is dressed more like a businessman than a footie fan, showing no England colours whatsoever. He offers us seats for both the Tunisia and Romania games.

'How much?'

'Two hundred and fifty for each game.'

'You're having a fucking laugh, ain't ya?'

He shrugs his shoulders, smiles and walks off. I turn to the two Spurs fans and explain that I would never pay that much just to watch one match hoping to find support. Unfortunately,

I can see in their eyes that they would have, and suddenly I feel alienated again.

I had arranged to travel the first part of the journey with one of my brothers, who was off to Paris to do some recording work with the singer Natalie Imbruglia. Greg has agreed to catch an earlier train so that he can be with me and put my mind at rest, but unfortunately he happens to be one of the world's great worriers and not really what I need at this moment. As we settle into our seats he informs me that he has heard all sorts of stories about Marseille and how violent it can be. Nice one bruv, I feel much better already.

As I start to reassure him about my safety the conversation makes me realise that I have left my driving licence at home and therefore will not be able to hire a car. This is a major bollock as I had intended that to be my safety net. I had in the back of my mind that if I couldn't find a hotel then at least I could crash out in the car, keeping all my gear tucked up safely in the boot at the same time. *Shit!*

Suddenly I begin to panic, and for a split second I decide that I will travel straight back home after the Tunisia game and just keep going back and forth using my five-day Euro-Domino train pass until England get knocked out. We pull into Lille, I get off and Greg heads off towards Paris, a top bit of Aussie crumpet and his nice comfy hotel. Bastard.

I have over an hour to kill before catching the TGV down to Marseille, so I desperately try to make friends. Like Waterloo, the place is busy with footie fans, travellers and coppers, only this time the Old Bill are carrying guns which make them look just that little bit harder than the traditional English bobby with a tit on his head. The 'Please, someone talk to me' neon sign that is obviously glowing brightly above my head drives everyone away to opposite corners of the station, except a couple of coppers who casually follow every move I make.

I go to the sandwich bar to escape their prying eyes and order a salad roll with no butter. The lady behind the counter hands over the egg roll and asks for more money than I had expected to pay. I think about trying to explain to her what being vegan means, but maybe this isn't quite the right place. I hold out my handful of change instead for her to pick at, and she takes even more than I expected. The smell of egg creeps up my nostrils telling me that I might just lose a little bit of weight on this trip.

I board the TGV, settle myself down and get myself comfortable just in time for the guard to rush on, order us off the train and onto another one waiting to go on the platform opposite. Croissants, baguettes and bottled water fly in all directions as the mad scramble that follows turns into a rush for window seats. Will this nightmare journey never end? Once more I settle myself down, only this time I keep all my belongings within snatching distance just in case. Ten minutes later the train shifts into motion and at last I can breathe a sigh of relief.

Sitting close by is the businessman I had seen at Waterloo with the tickets. I can't help wondering whether I can beat him up or not, lifting all his tickets in the process. Well, I am only human; we all think like that in times of need, don't we? *Don't we?* Surely there must be a few other lads on this train in the same boat who wouldn't mind lending a hand? Eventually I think better of it. He may well be a homicidal maniac and I've got enough to worry about as it is, so I strike up conversation with the couple sitting opposite.

Trevor and Pat are in their late fifties and come from Rainham in Kent. Trevor works for the rail company Connex South East, which, he tells me, is a French-owned business. Last Monday he entered a free World Cup draw being run for company employees, and on Thursday was told that he had struck gold. Trevor's prize is a three-day trip to Marseille including top hotels, hospitality at the stadium and free match tickets for him and the lovely Pat. What a complete bastard. As everyone earwigs the conversation he goes on to inform us that he doesn't really like football that much any more and had wanted to sell the prize on. Unbelievably, Trevor was a bit pissed off as one of his colleagues had offered him £600 to take the prize off his hands but the company bosses would have none of it, so he and Pat were just going to enjoy it for what it was, a freebie. Fuck me, some people are never happy, are they? Suddenly I want to beat up Trevor and Pat more than the businessman with the tickets, but she does the mumsy thing and offers me a boiled sweet by way of compensation, so I put all thoughts of murder to the back of my mind.

As the train heads south more people join the conversation. The lad on the table next to us is Dave, off to visit his girlfriend who has been at university in Marseille for the past year. Dave is the first person I have ever met with something good to say about the Mediterranean port. He puts a few minds at rest by telling us where and where not to go in the city.

The conversation soon turns to other things such as the topic of the worst job you have ever had. I think I lift the prize by telling them that I was once employed to pick weeds out of the bunkers at the local golf course, when suddenly Trevor and Dave find that they have something dark and nasty in common. Both had once held the position as chief burner of body parts at their local hospital incinerator unit. The carriage falls silent as Dave informs us that the worst thing he ever scorched was a little baby's hand. Now I am very scared, more scared than I have ever been in my life. I just want to get off the train and away from these people as quickly as is humanly possible.

I don't want to talk to Trevor any more. I don't even want to risk him catching me looking, so I turn my attention back to my newspaper. While flicking through I read an item stating that FIFA had ordered all the referees to attend the opening game, only for the men in black to turn up and find that the governing body had forgot to provide them with match tickets. Funny, yes, but it doesn't exactly fill me with hope of finding tickets either.

As the TGV speeds south I try to sit back, relax and enjoy the journey. While I gaze out of the window and take in the scenery, the fair city I am heading for has been transformed into a battle zone. For some the war zone is welcome; for others it's a nightmare. Mike from Middlesbrough certainly didn't like what he saw:

We had been staying out of the city on a camp site some ten miles away. Everywhere we went the locals were saying, 'Your English hooligans are coming to fight with the Tunisian fans, yes?' and it really began to get to you after the hundredth time. We had been looking forward to this for months, but that constant reminder of what was expected had us all heads down and apprehensive rather than excited. We kept asking ourselves the same question, as did some of the locals we spoke to: Why England v. Tunisia here? Of all places, why Marseille?

We went to the city early that day to soak up the sun and suss the place out, and at first the feeling was much better than we had expected. The English were there in their thousands, kitted out in the colours, drinking and soaking up the sun. The Tunisian fans were doing the same, having a meal and a laugh, and at that stage mixing well with the English. The problem was all the young local kids walking around in little groups. They were cocky little so-and-so's. You'd be sitting at your table minding your own business and one would walk right past you and start mouthing off. As the afternoon moved on you could tell the English lads were getting more drunk and more pissed off. It was only a matter of time before it kicked off, and even now I ask myself why we didn't just get up and leave. I suppose I can only put it down to morbid curiosity. Sure enough, up it went.

Why? Well, many reasons, I think. No one can deny that the locals were baiting the England fans. They were as willing and organised as any fans I've ever seen looking for trouble, but when it happened they quickly found themselves outnumbered as all the England lads took it on. As much as you have to blame the locals you have to blame the English. There always looked to be little mobs wandering around ready to go, but once it went off there seemed more like about 300, and they went for it all right. I've seen plenty of this before following England and back home, and most of the time it looks far worse than it actually is, just people running and glass smashing, but this was different. When people start running past you with blood dripping from their heads after being hit by a bottle, eyes and noses split after being smashed in the face, it gets scary.

At first the police were taken as well and the English lads gave them a fair running, beating up anyone they could. Usually if you want to get out of the way you can, but here there were so many innocent people that it was almost impossible. Once the police came back in things got worse. They were quick to fire the teargas making it worse for the innocent fans and firing up the violent ones even more. Then the Tunisians came back in and suddenly you started to see people lying on the floor and blood everywhere. That was when I started to panic. One guy ran past saying he had been cut and that the Tunisians were carrying knives, and of course people go mad then. The thing was that he wasn't lying, and you knew it. The England lads kept charging forward, mostly at the police, which was mad. The Tunisians seemed to be everywhere. First they'd be up one side street throwing bottles and stones, then once they were chased they'd appear at the next street doing the same thing.

I have to say the police seemed more bothered about the English than the locals, but that is probably because the English lads stayed around the same area and it was easier to pick them off, which is fair enough I suppose. All the bars were getting turned over, windows put through and chairs smashed.

Somehow we found ourselves up a side street by a small square just as a group of local lads came round the corner. They were hitting out at anyone in an England shirt; old, young, it didn't matter. I wanted to get out of the way, so I shot into this little bar restaurant just as the owner ran out to see what was going on. He shit himself and told us to get inside so that he could shut the doors. I didn't need asking twice and just stood and watched as some poor guy got kicked half to death. It is a horrible experience having to stand by and watch what I honestly thought was someone being killed. Something must have happened around the corner because they suddenly all ran as if scared by something. But one last Tunisian kid took his chance and smashed a wooden chair right down on this bloke. Even I felt that, but the body on the floor just shook.

Then a few bottles smashed on the floor where the Tunisians had just been fighting, and some English lads appeared. I asked the owner to let me and my mate out, which he did, but once outside we didn't have a clue where to go and so just ran back in the direction of where the English lads had come from. The problem then is that to the police you look like a hooligan and can well end up getting battered yourself. All this had been going on for about an hour before we managed to get well away. It took us another ten minutes to get up to the station, but all the way you felt that if you crossed the wrong person you could end up getting stabbed or badly beaten up. In fact it was almost more scary walking up to the station than being shut in the bar, because up here you were really on your own.

That hour was one of the most frightening I have ever had because even little kids seemed to be at it. The one thing I did learn was that next time I am away with England and it starts to look dodgy I won't be hanging around.

Whereas Mike wanted away, for others this was what they had been waiting for. DD of LCFC enjoyed every minute:

What most people, coppers and politicians don't get is that when you're away with England you're on duty. Every day, every minute. We had been waiting for this since the final whistle blew in Italy and we qualified, and we didn't let ourselves or our country down. We went to Marseille and proved to the world yet again just who the top dogs are. England turned up and did a job. Not like the Germans, the Dutch or the Italians who shit out of Euro '96. We turned up and took it to them, on their soil, and that's how you show the rest who's top.

We ran those filthy bastards everywhere. They'd given it the big one all day, mouthing at scarfers, families and nobodies, but when we went for it they shit out. Like every other country the bottle went, and I'll never forget the look on their frightened faces when the England lads came together. They were fuck all – kids throwing bottles and carrying knives. They never wanted to fight, not once, they just ran like fuck every time. Marseille, the most violent city on the Mediterranean. Well it was that day, because England had come to town and we took the place over. A little bit of England, won with English bottle.

And what about the French police? Fucking shitters. We heard so much beforehand, didn't we? How hard they were, terrorist training, all that shit. They ran. When it first kicked off they ran, just like the local lads. It makes me laugh. They've got dogs, batons and guns and we still had them on their toes.

Marseille was the best buzz I've had in years. We put ourselves well and truly back at the top that day because every lad in the world would have seen the England lads in action on foreign soil. See, that's the thing, doing it there. They were at home, so it was down to them to bring it to us, but they didn't have the bottle. We turned up, gave them the chance and ended up doing it ourselves, and to the lads that's taking the piss. I'll never forget

running down that street, standing tall as the riot police
fired the teargas and then kicking it back. There were so
many lads there wanting to mix it it was unreal, lads
with real bottle doing it for their country. Why can't they
just once have it with us toe to toe?

'Course, back home the press will have us as scum
and the politicians will want us hanging. They will tell
the country they should hate us, be ashamed of us and
be ashamed to be English. If you're not proud to be
English then I couldn't give a fuck what you think. They
kid themselves if they think people hate us. Deep inside
most lads love it, most people love it. They love talking
about it at work or in the pub. They can't wait to hear
what we got up to, who done what, who got nicked or
who got battered. They want to know what it was really
like. It makes me die when the press put our pictures in
the paper hoping to shame people. OK, so no one needs
that, but if you happen to be one of the unlucky ones
and it's your face on the page then you live with it for a
few days. Joe Public soon forgets, but the lads that
matter don't.

We're proud of our country, proud of what we are. I
am sick and tired of the rest of the world treating us like
dirt. I am sick of being seen as the doormat of Europe.
The people that run our country should be ashamed of
themselves for giving away so much of what our fathers
fought for. They have forgotten what we as a country
did for the world. They would rather teach our kids about
American history than our own, and that sickens me. I'll
fight for England wherever I can. I won't stand by and
do nothing if some shitty Arab throws a bottle at a
restaurant full of innocent people, or rides past on a bike
and cuts up one of my own. I am proud of all those lads
prepared to front a line of riot police who only want to
defend their own rather than protect the innocent. If they
have something to prove then we're English, we're here,
let's prove it.

When I get back home I hold my head up high. Too many people don't give a fuck any more; thankfully, many of those that follow England do. Keep writing the headlines, the books and showing the film on the news; it puts us on the map and gets the message over. The message – English and proud.

By including that letter from DD I will once again be laying myself open to the criticism that I am glorifying violence, but you can only find a solution to a problem if you understand what drives people in the first place.

While the views of those actually caught up in the violence differed greatly, the British press only had eyes, ears and shocking headlines to reflect one side of the story. In the *Mirror* newspaper the following day, the comment section 'Voice of the *Mirror*' left us in no doubt as to the stance the paper wanted to take:

The fans of 32 nations are gathered in France for the world's greatest sporting celebration. But only ours riot. Only ours launch into day-long battles with the police. Only ours think that fighting is better than football.

Whoever it was that penned those words may well have written something a little closer to the truth if they had bothered to read the reports written by their own journalists beforehand. Under the headlines 'MADMEN OF MARSEILLE' and 'A BLOODY DISGRACE', Jeremy Armstrong and Steven Atkinson produced further one-sided articles. However, reading between the lines there are a few little gems of information that may have balanced the argument. The front page started with:

England was shamed last night as soccer thugs went on a rampage of violence in Marseille. More than one hundred were arrested after ugly clashes with rival supporters and French riot police on the eve of our opening World Cup match against Tunisia.

'I walked into the nightmare of England fans hurling missiles, glasses and bottles at their Tunisian rivals. They [the Tunisians] replied by letting off fireworks and throwing petrol bombs . . .'

No doubt about the fact that the English nation was shamed, but were all those arrested English? And while the English were hurling missiles, where did all those petrol bombs and fireworks suddenly materialise from? These articles are written in such a way that they lead the reader into thinking that only the English fans came prepared. The letter from DD provides more than enough evidence that many Englishmen did arrive in the city looking for trouble, but there is no demand from this paper for the French or Tunisian governments to act to curb their fans.

The paper adds: 'The riot police formed a line, moving forward and beating their shields in a desperate attempt to bring order.' In all my days I have never seen such action restore order. The banging of shields by riot police officers is often taken as an act of provocation. Threatening violence, not calming it.

The pages are full of quotes. These come from English fans who often remain anonymous, while those from the Tunisians and French carry names, something I always find highly dubious. One Tunisian, Majhid Bouzbhi, claimed to have been threatened with a knife, while an unnamed guest of a hotel describes a different incident:

'This guy came up and attacked him and slashed him with a knife across the throat. He looked like a Tunisian. The lad who was injured appeared to be in a bad way. The English fans shouted at the police to chase after him but they did not react quickly enough, and that caused even bigger trouble.'

It's the last few words that attract the attention, insinuating that the English fans went into a frenzy. Just what was this 'even bigger trouble' the reporter quotes? An England fan did have his throat slashed that day, and it's true the police didn't do their job.

Unless you have personally witnessed something like that you can never understand the range of emotions you experience. I've seen something not far different, and I wouldn't recommend it. At first you're scared shitless because it could have been you, and you want to get away as quick as possible, but your legs won't move. You want to help the victim and at the same time you want the bastard caught. If the police are there you expect justice, and if it doesn't come you get fucking angry and want revenge. In this incident the guy with the knife doesn't get slaughtered, the police action doesn't get questioned, yet the English fans getting the hump finishes it all off nicely.

The pages also treat us to some shocking photographs supported by even more shocking captions. One reads: 'HATE: An England supporter screams defiance as the police close in on the mob.' The picture actually shows one guy with blood pouring from both a head wound and a cut chin. Admittedly, he appears to be shouting and is giving it the two fingers, but he isn't with a mob and there are definitely no police closing in. Now, I don't know this guy from Adam. For all I know he might be a complete fruit-bat who eats kids for fun, but he looks more like a bloke who has just been hit on the head with a bottle, has fallen over and hit his chin, and is feeling a little pissed off with life.

Another caption reads: 'One yob gives a Nazi salute and another sets fire to a Tunisian flag before the fighting in Marseille yesterday evening.' This picture clearly shows a group of lads burning the Tunisian flag, which I agree is a truly aggressive and despicable act. But Nazi-saluting Englishmen can't be seen. One lad has his arm out straight, hand flat, but the caption writer chooses to ignore the fact that the other arm is doing exactly the same. Now buy me a new cowboy outfit if I am wrong, but I never saw row after row of Nazis marching along, both arms out, forming a 'Y' shape and looking like a load of Village People groupies. The lad in that picture could get tainted for life by bad caption writing, yet this is the lazy journalism that Mr and Mrs Average lap up.

Back on the train, and oblivious to all this, I decide to stretch my legs and go for a walk. In doing so I bump into Glenn Fedorowicz, a 43-year-old Polish-American from Chicago. Like every American I've met, Glenn likes to talk, and to my surprise he knows his football:

My parents are Polish Jews who headed for America after the war. My father was a good footballer and probably could have played at league level if he had stayed back home, but in America the game just wasn't taken seriously at that time. When he arrived in the States there were plenty of ethnic soccer teams, but it was all very local. It didn't take long for him to find other Poles who wanted to form their own team, and that side is still running today.

I was brought up around that team and so played soccer all through my childhood. Dad taught me to play as soon as I could stand up. Dad was a really good coach and was sure that one day soccer was going to take off big in the States. I suppose like all fathers he wanted his son to be a star and live out his dreams for him, so he coached me so that I would have a head start on all the American kids. Actually, his effort paid off because I ended up playing in the Pro-Indoor League for Albuquerque Gunners and Denver Kickers before going on to train as a coach myself, which is what I do now, coaching kids in Chicago. It's taken a little longer than we both expected, but soccer has at last taken hold and you will find a soccer ball as well as an American football and baseball in most kids' backyards now, which is great.

I am sure you know that the most important thing in the States is money, and following on from USA '94 people have realised there is plenty of it to be made in soccer. We have realised where the game went wrong with the old Major League set-up. Too many old-timers were brought over for a last big pay cheque, so teams went bust, but this time round they have put a wage cap on the players' earnings which will help keep the running costs down and more teams in business. It also stops too many players from coming over and stuffing big pay cheques in their pockets for little return, and encourages American youngsters to come through, which is vitally important to the American people. They like to see their own achieving back in the States. Last time round New York Cosmos was the only team to really make any money. That was because New York is full of ethnics like me, people from countries who understood and knew the game back then. Pele may well have been the greatest player in the world to us, but the American public was only just finding out about the game he played, let alone who its major stars were.

Sport is big, big business back in the States, and TV runs the show. Soccer runs on the same franchise system as American football, which you Brits find hard to understand as soccer is seen as more of a representation of a city or area. Back home there will probably be fewer than forty teams in the Major League once it's established properly, and if a team isn't pulling in the crowds, the advertising revenue or the viewing figures that the TV stations want to see, then the franchise will be sold off to the highest bidder and shipped out overnight. Wham, your soccer team gone just like that. Unfortunately for the fans, America is a big place so they can get away with it. It happens all the time in every other sport and soccer will be no different.

After five and a half hours the TGV finally pulls into the station at Marseille. As I get off the train the worry of finding somewhere to stay grips me again as hundreds of England fans swarm around the platform. I head off towards the tourist information office and join the long queue of those looking for hotels. To my surprise the line moves quickly, but I soon find out why. The stories doing the rounds about rioting English fans have turned out to be true, so if you are English you've no chance of finding a hotel for the night. Bollocks. I really don't need to hear that.

For some reason I decide to stay in the queue. Even the happy couple at the desk are turned away as the flustered woman behind the counter repeats the same eight words. 'There are no hotels taking English people, sorry.' As I get to the front the phone rings, her eyes light up and the room falls quiet.

'I have one room for four people.'

Re-fucking-sult! As I am next in the queue I look around for another three punters. Two right behind me, lovely. I need one more, but next in line is another couple.

'Will they let five in the room?' I ask.

'No.'

Fair enough, that's them out of the race then. I shout out for one more but get no reply as everyone is in groups of two. The woman behind the desk is getting desperate, and so am I. I apologise to the lads directly behind me as I happily sentence them to the dangers of the street. 'Sorry lads, but you know how it is. OK then. Have we got a group of three?' Silence. Oh for fuck's sake. I have no choice but to let the next four lads have the room, so I pick up my bag and storm out.

As I barge through the door I moan at the top of my voice, 'There must be some other idiot here on his own!'

Then a voice pipes up. 'Yeah, I'm on me own, mate.'

I look round to see a large, rather nasty-looking cropped-haired bloke.

'You looking for a room?' I ask hopefully.

'Yeah, why, you got one?'

'Yes I fucking have.' I bundle myself back into the office

and re-stake my claim for the room. 'Sorry lads, but I've found another bloke to share with, and as I was first in the queue and all that.'

One of the lads from the second group of two is not so keen on my request. 'Oh come off it, mate, you gave it to us four.'

'Yeah, I know, but now I've hooked up with him, ain't I?' My new room-mate pokes his head around the door right on cue, and yes, he is still nasty-looking. I can see the lad visibly thinking over the possible repercussions in his mind.

'Are we in then?' says my new room-mate.

I look once more at the lad, who has now begun to flinch.

'Yeah, I think so.'

I soon learn that my new room-mate is a Man Utd fan from Kent but watches most of his football at Herne Bay. I would like to refer to him as the EMU (Exiled Man Utd fan), but daren't as he might just rip my head off. His voice is as aggressive as his looks, and I can't help but think that he could well turn out to be a very handy bloke to be hooked up with. From now on he shall be known as Herne Bay (HB).

We book the room and head off to catch the Metro along with our fellow room-mates, Paul and Mick. These two are from Reading and Newport Pagnell respectively and appear to be just a couple of average blokes who are into their football. Paul supports Tottenham while Mick follows Arsenal. They both tell me that they watch most of their football via Sky these days as tickets are hard to come by and too expensive. Both follow England live whenever they can instead. As we make for the escalator two more lads come over, introduce themselves and ask if it's OK for them to tag along with us and see whether the hotel has an additional room available. Herne Bay tells them that if not they can just bunk in with us, and at this stage what HB says is fine by me.

The hotel is much posher than any of us had expected, and pretty soon we are checked in and up in the room fighting for the beds. Herne Bay goes back down with the key before returning with the other two lads who were looking for a room. 'The bird on reception knows the score. These two will be all right crashing in here with us,' he announces. It turns out that these two are also from Kent, which I am beginning to think must be the hot bed of English football support. Forget all about the north-east, Merseyside, the Midlands or London, you want to get down to the Garden of England, pal, that's where your real football passion lies. Dartford, Maidstone, Thanet.

One of the lads, Gary, looks like the bass player out of Level 42 and is constantly on about getting hold of a packet of cigarettes, while the other, whom I will refer to as Mr B, looks like a hippy. As the rest of us argue over who's next in the shower, Mr B heads off to the toilet and starts making all sorts of horrible noises. Five minutes later he returns with reddened cheeks and beads of sweat on his brow. I had to say something.

'Bloody hell, you must have needed to get that out.'

'No, I didn't have a dump, I needed to get this out.' Between his fingers Mr B is swinging what looks like a second-hand Durex.

'What the fuck's that?'

'I brought a couple of grams of cocaine over with me.'

Me, Paul and Mick look on in disbelief, while Gary cracks up. 'Well, he is on holiday after all.' Herne Bay walks in, gets told the story and cracks up as well.

I can't help but try and work out what Paul and Mick must be making of all this. Sharing the same room is just about all we have in common, and as far as tickets go our circumstances couldn't be more different. Mick and Paul are only out for this one game, and while Mick has a ticket, Paul hasn't. Herne Bay has tickets for every England game as well as vouchers for every England match all the way to the final, but unfortunately for him he is having to go back and forth for each game as he can't get the time off work. Mr B and Gary are staying out and have one ticket each, but for them the shitter is that Mr B's ticket is for the Romania game in Toulouse, while Gary's is for the match against Colombia in Lens. Obviously no chance of sitting next to your mate at a game then. Of all the people in the room I am the only one who is not a member of the Official England Travel Club, which explains my predicament. Paul, although a member, hasn't got a ticket because he hasn't been to enough England matches under that 'official banner' to qualify for one yet. What a shambles. I ask Herne Bay how he managed to get tickets all the way to the final:

I go to watch England every game, home and away, and I've been in the travel club for years. At first, when I applied they sent me tickets for all the first-round games, but only semi-final and final vouchers. I went fucking mental. I got on the phone and gave them a right mouthful, telling them that I'd been to every game, about all the ones I'd done officially. I told them I'd go to the papers, everything. I am one of the diehard fans, you see. If they would have stitched me up some of the others would have had the right hump an' all. I told them I'd leave the travel club and get a load of others to as well. They told me they'd look into it and see what they could do, and the next day I had the rest of the vouchers land on my doormat. You can't just take the shit off these people: if you don't have a go back then they think they can just keep doing it. As soon as the vouchers arrived I rang a mate who had the same thing done to him. He got straight on the blower, gave them the same verbal and bosh, next day he got the vouchers as well.

He then goes on to tell us about some of the more lively trips abroad he has had with England, including the fact that he has been deported from three countries while following his country: Ireland, Sweden and Norway. And this is the lad who got tickets from the FA all the way to the final.

Here's a tip when travelling abroad with England. If there's a group of you and you're all mates you should always leave your passports in the hotel safe deposit box. If you get lifted they just want to ship you out as soon as.

If they can't get your passport then they can't formally identify you and that way no one gets to find out. You'll get a bit of grief off the British Embassy people if they come down, but you just stick it out. And if one of the lads you're with keeps out of the way, he then brings all the passports back home with him. I never go looking for it, I done all that when I was younger, but sometimes you don't have to look, do you, it comes to you. I won't be getting in any hassle out here because I've got my tickets, and I ain't going to risk missing out.

As I've noted down before, Herne Bay is a Man Utd fan, and so it would follow that he lives hundreds of miles away from Old Trafford. I have to admit that in the past I've taken my fair share of pops at supporters like that as I've always felt you should support the club on your doorstep, no matter who it is (and yes, that does include Luton), but Herne Bay soon set me straight and had me begging forgiveness:

I've supported Man Utd since I was a kid. As soon as I was old enough I went to every game I could, home and away. There are loads of lads down our way who do the same. I was travelling all the way up from Kent for every home game, and I mean every home game when Man Utd were shit. There is one lad down our way who runs a minibus to every game, and it's always full. He hasn't missed a United game since 1969. Now, are you telling me that just because he doesn't live in Manchester he is any less of a supporter? He has to put up with that bollocks all the time, just as I did. I would spend all my wages on following United. It would have been much easier to follow my local side and it would have saved me a fucking fortune, but I support Man Utd so I watch Man Utd.

I know there are thousands of glory hunters out there but it fucks you off when everyone has a go at you before they take the time to find out. Like most blokes, I went through that stage of settling down and couldn't afford to go for a while, and then you find out you've gone to the back of the queue. I am as pissed off with those people as anyone because now I can't get tickets. You can't ring up the ticket office at Old Trafford and have a go because they can afford to put the phone down on you. They couldn't give a toss because they know they could sell their tickets five times over.

Now I do follow my local side, Herne Bay, but people still take the piss. You can't win. People think they're not a proper side because they ain't in the league. Well it's the same thing: there are old boys down there who haven't missed a game for years and years. They do the pitch, paint the stands, they're the salt of the earth, fucking diamonds. If it wasn't for them the club would have folded years ago. They really do support the club and in a way that no supporter of a big club could possibly hope to. I love it down there.

I still go to watch United a few times a season, but only if I can sit with me mates and have a laugh. I don't want to sit next to people I don't know. At Herne Bay you know everyone. You can slag the manager off to his face if we lose, or buy him a beer if we win. As much as I love Man Utd and the big-match atmosphere, I can see football killing itself. Following England is going the same way; you only have to look at the tickets us lot have. We're all over the place, ain't we!

Herne Bay's experience is not unique as more and more supporters turn to their local non-league club after being screwed by their first love. For R.M.C. that move was easy. He saw the way football was heading a few years before the rest of us. I was sent this letter in August 1997:

Remember when Palace were suddenly billed as the team of the eighties and everybody wanted to jump on the bandwagon? Well, there were some of us who had followed them for a few years before that, but when all that happened the club didn't give a monkeys. I don't know of any other club that has fucked its supporters around as much as Palace, and in the end I'd had enough. I am Palace through and through, always will be until the day I die. That is the only thing they can't take from me. But as far as the people that run the club are concerned I am just another bod, £15 or whatever it is now every other Saturday.

It all started on that famous, or as I call it infamous, day when 52,000 turned up to watch Palace beat Burnley 2–0. We knew it was going to be a big crowd – it was the promotion celebration game after all – but it seemed that the whole of Norbury, Croydon, Selhurst and Thornton Heath had suddenly become Palace and everyone wanted their little bit of the glory. What really fucked me off that day was that we couldn't see a thing or get near the pitch. We were the lads who travelled to Grimsby, a shit hole that smells of fish where you can catch piles by sitting on their shitty wooden benches. We were the lads that had run the gauntlet at toilets like Cardiff, and when the moment came we never saw a thing as our lads gained promotion. There was a lot of resentment among the faithful as we knew we would never see a crowd like that again, but the club never once admitted it cocked things up and never said sorry to its loyal supporters. They sold us off that day in the hope of pulling in a few extra punters.

The next nail in the coffin for me was when they sold off part of the ground to Sainsbury's. That part of the ground was the traditional away end with the home terrace being the Holmesdale Road End. To counter the loss of terracing they then section off a third of our end and give it to the away fans. We went up the wall. Football clubs just don't have a clue about the fans and how they feel about their ground. We couldn't believe that just like that they had given away something Palace fans had spent years defending. We got so pissed off at having to go through that every home game that we decided to move off into the Arthur Waite Enclosure, but unbelievably the club then gave over a section of that to the away fans as well. Every week we were pelted with coins and stones, but whenever we had a go the police piled in on us and just let them get on with it. It was like the club just never wanted us and pushed us around whenever they felt like it. Then we have the ground shares with Charlton and Wimbledon – it's like the place don't belong to us any more.

A few years back I moved down to Kent [another one!] and to tell you the truth I was getting well pissed off with the whole thing. One by one the lads I went with were beginning to pick their games as the prices were getting stupid, so I started to go and watch my local side, Ramsgate. I got so involved in the club that in my second season I got awarded supporter of the year. I think this is what football is all about now. We've got Spurs, Chelsea, ex-ICF and Bushwhackers, and a few Gunners as well. We pull each other's legs all the time, but at the end of the day we all follow the Rams and have a right laugh. I was nominated by the supporters onto the committee, and for the first time in donkey's years I really felt part of a football club instead of a never-ending wallet to tap.

I still get to Palace a few times, but sitting in the two-tiered wedding cake they call the home end just isn't the same. Give me the old Holmesdale End back any day. It also really hurts me to see the Arthur Waite Stand given over to the away fans. He might not mean a lot to the new fans or directors, but to the rest of us that man was a hero. Seeing away fans sitting in the stand dedicated to that man and having them give us a lot of abuse is just too much.

The final straw for me is seeing all these new celebrity fans. I don't mind Ronnie Corbett, Roger De Courcey or

David Jensen because they have been there since as long as I can remember, and they stayed through the bad times. But when I see Eddie Izzard turn up wearing make-up and looking like my Gran in drag it makes me sick. Why put him on the telly when you want to speak to a Palace fan? Why not get a proper bloke? People like him make the club a laughing stock. The more I see of things like that the more it makes me want to be back at Ramsgate. We have a beer, mix with the away fans, stand on the terraces and take the piss out of each other. That's what football should be like.

I tell Herne Bay about this letter, and just to prove that the rivalry is just as severe at this level he gives me his opinion on his county rivals: 'Ramsgate: shit ground, shit fans, shit team. What else do you want to know?'

Gary flicks through the TV channels to track down some football. We soon find out that Argentina have scraped a 1–0 win over the Japs thanks to a goal from Batistuta, while Yugoslavia have won by the same score against Iran, both teams looking none too convincing. We are then treated to pictures of Japanese fans clearing up all the litter from the stadium and placing it into black plastic bags; apparently, when they win they go round to the opposing supporters' houses and do their ironing as well.

Back home, the England team players are indulging in one of those wacky games they love so much. It has been decided among the camp that in order to spice up live interviews the players must try to include a song title in the answers they give to any question! Gareth Southgate was beside himself when managing to work in 'Club Tropicana' by Wham! What crazy guys those footballers are!

Now the time has come for us to venture out onto the streets of Marseille and find a nice quiet bar in time to watch Jamaica play Croatia. As Gary, Mr B and I are staying out in France, we re-book the room for the following night so as to save us the hassle of looking for somewhere new in the morning. They also tell me that they hope to hook up with another mate of theirs at the ground tomorrow called Tony, who could jump in with us and keep the cost down if I am willing. Mr B tells me that I'll like Tony as he's 'a one off'. Gary starts to laugh. I can't help wondering why I'll like Tony so much, as being 'a one off' obviously means something different down Kent way – at least I hope it does!

As we walk down the main drag the sound of police sirens can be heard ringing out in the distance. Within five minutes we find ourselves standing outside the main police station and park ourselves down in the bar opposite. Everyone we speak to tells us of trouble kicking off all day around the port area, and that it is best to give it a miss. On hearing this Gary and Mr B immediately want to go down and take a look. The main form of entertainment comes via the steady to and fro of police vans carrying Englishmen to the cells opposite the bar. Amazingly, Herne Bay bumps into the Man Utd supporter he told us about who drives the minibus from Kent to every game at Old Trafford, so we stay for a second beer before heading off down the road and towards the port.

We only have to walk about 200 yards when we find another quiet drinking hole situated on a main crossroads and full of England fans, both men and women. As the lads take a table outside I go in to order the beers. I order the last six bottles of beer in the house when all of a sudden the bar fills up as people come rushing in. At first I think it's a mad dash for the bar as the beer appears to be running out, but the lad next to me lets me know the worst. A large mob is heading this way and they are not English. The bastard barman snatches the money from my hand just as the first window goes through, then he disappears down behind the counter.

Suddenly the noise becomes deafening as more glass smashes and people begin shouting and running in all directions. Experience tells me that at times like this it is always better to be out in the open rather than trapped inside, so I too make a hasty exit while desperately trying to keep hold of six bottles of beer. In the chaos outside Gary and Mr B are the only two people I manage to spot. As I join them the battle is in full swing. About 20 yards down from the far corner of the crossroads is a mob of around 60 lads. These lads are obviously not English and appear to be made up of French, Tunisian and Arab kids. They are throwing anything they can get their hands on in the direction of the bar, and their aim is almost akin to that of Eric Bristow. Some of the English lads have mobbed up and are giving back just as good as they are getting. Every time the English lads run forward the locals leg it, then once all the missiles have been thrown the locals come back chucking more stuff of their own.

You can tell that the majority of the people in this bar are just out for a beer rather than a night out on the town looking for a row. It is also obvious that this is never going to turn into anything more than a throwing session as the locals keep enough distance so as to avoid getting a punch or a kick up the arse. Despite that, it has to be said that this little mob knows exactly what it is doing. One lumbering fat lad seems to be pulling the strings along with a thin lad wearing a blue track-suit, whom I later find out was one of the top lads at the local side, Olympic Marseille. It must also be noted that these lads have bottle and plenty of it, and to be honest I am glad that there are a few lads around prepared to have a go back, else they could overrun the place and probably hurt a fair few people.

A small fire bomb is thrown towards the bar by one of the locals. Thankfully it falls short and explodes in the middle of the road junction. It can't be petrol as the flames would have spread out across the road, but the flames light up the scene nonetheless and bring with them an even heavier atmosphere. Time and again the English lads run them back only for them to turn and do the off, but I have no doubt that these locals know what they are doing. Every time they back off it gives the English fans still trapped inside the chance to get themselves clear.

Slowly but surely the numbers diminish and the English become too few to hold their ground. On seeing this the local lads start to edge closer towards the bar. Now when they launch their bottles and broken chairs at us less and less is being offered in return, and very soon it becomes one-way traffic. At this point I, for one, have seen enough and the time has come to take the fastest walk I have ever made back in the direction of the hotel. As the locals finally take over the bar they let out a triumphant cheer.

There were two things that really struck me about this incident. Firstly I was amazed by the age of the locals as their mob appeared to be made up mostly of teenagers and young kids. The second thought that stuck in my mind was the noticeable absence of the local Old Bill. As I've said, this bar was just 250 yards down from the local cop shop, and while this whole incident must have gone on for about five solid minutes not one copper put in an appearance. This despite the fact that from where they were stationed you could clearly see the junction where all this had taken place.

As me, Gray and Mr B duck down a side road we can't help but feel a little pissed off at the events we have just witnessed, and now we don't really have a clue where we are heading. In this part of the city the roads seem to run on some kind of grid system and every junction has the old butterflies going as you never know what you could come face to face with. On turning one corner we receive a clear view down towards what we later find out is the port. In the distance all you can see is flashing blue lights, running bodies and smoke, at which point we make probably one of our better decisions of the night and turn around to head back to where we have just come from. We take another turning to find a group of locals, no more than twelve years old, beating the metal front of a shop with a paving slab. Eventually we get back on the main drag and head back up towards the bar opposite the cop shop.

As we walk we bump into a small group of lads walking in the opposite direction. We tell them that they'd be better off turning around, but they're having none of it. 'No way. This ain't over yet. We're going to see if we can pick off a few of the stragglers.'

As we talk I find out they are from Exeter, one of them a guy who had written to me on more than one occasion, a good lad but obviously a little mad in wanting to finish off his evening with a stroll back to the port.

Back at the bar everyone is buzzing and talking about what they have seen. It turns out that those local lads have been at it all day. For most of the day they have been chased all over the place, but now, as the majority of the English fans have made for their hotels or been nicked, the locals are at last enjoying having the upper hand. Rumours are flying around that some of the local Arab kids were riding around on scooters with a passenger on the back. The passengers were said to be carrying blades and slashing out at people as they drove past. With this story being told by more than one person, I decide to stand an extra few feet back from the kerb. Many others are also talking about people being stabbed, mugged and badly beaten while walking down side streets, and I begin to wonder why I am here and whether I would actually see my wife again. I am really risking all this just to see a football match!

Eventually me and the lads begin thinking that this bar could well be the next one to come under attack, so we finish our beers and head off in the hope of finding another bar. As luck would have it the Holiday Inn is situated conveniently en route to the hotel. As well as being prepared to serve such a motley crew it also provides a few extra little moments of interest as I find myself standing shoulder to shoulder with Alan, who happens to be a journalist for that great British institution know as the *Sun* newspaper.

We've been down at the port today, and it was fantastic until about three o'clock, then it all went right off. It was stupid. We'd had Melinda Messenger down there with us all day. We were going around on the tour bus and everyone was loving it. We'd given hats out, Melinda was being great and signing stuff. Everyone was having a great time and then the bottles started flying and the police came on all heavy-handed. They were well over the top on the English lads. We were going to take Melinda out with us again tomorrow, but it's all got so heavy that we want to get her back to England and out of here as soon as possible. I am actually flying back with her at about noon tomorrow. We were going to take her out to Toulouse as well, but I don't think her agent will allow that now.

As Gary desperately tries to find out the lovely Melinda's room number, me and Mr B tell Alan about our night out on the tiles. Mr B then asks him what his newspaper is likely to be saying about the England fans come tomorrow morning.

Something deep inside tells me that Alan is desperately looking for a way out on this one, so I leave him at the bar to find Herne Bay in a heated argument with a Coventry City fan who has taken exception to the fact that my room-mate is an exiled Man Utd fan. Vast amounts of alcohol have not only loosened the Midlander's tongue but must also have seriously affected his eyesight. He stands about three stone and six inches smaller than my friend from Kent, and appears to be oblivious to the fact that Herne Bay is quickly becoming very pissed off. A serious beating appears to be just a few seconds away.

The television sports reporter Ray Stubbs then enters the bar. Herne Bay can't quite place his face and asks him what he does for a living. 'I ask people stupid questions,' replies a rather sarcastic Stubbsy, a side swipe I find to be highly amusing.

The Sky Sports team puts in a late appearance and the talking bollocks rises to a new level. Listening to all their bullshit I soon become convinced that these news crews, in their desperation to outdo each other, sensationalise events so much that they actually begin to believe the crap they spout. Before I decide to leave I ask one reporter whether he knows the final score of the Jamaican game. He tells me Croatia won 3–1 but I don't know if I actually believe him or not.

'Ere we go, 'Ere we go, 'Ere we go . . . Oh no!

As I walk back towards my hotel alone I can't help thinking that saying goodbye to my wife seems like weeks ago rather than a matter of just under twenty hours. Let's hope tomorrow is a little less stressful.

Life's A Beach
Day 6: Monday, 15 June

The day starts early due to the fact that not one of us had managed to obtain a match ticket while out on our travels the previous night. One of the lads tells us that he heard a rumour about an American ticket agency based down near the port area behind an Irish bar. They are supposedly having a large amount of tickets delivered today, so it is decided that after breakfast we will head off in that direction.

Back up in the room we are getting ourselves together when Herne Bay enters and tells me that he has just been given the room number of a bloke who has a spare ticket for sale. I call the number to be told that he has one hospitality ticket going for £100. He goes on to tell me that the ticket belongs to his dad who has been put off by all the trouble and would now rather watch it in the hotel bar. One hundred pounds doesn't seem that bad a deal, but something tells me not to take up the offer. I don't like all that corporate stuff at the best of times, or paying over the odds for tickets, so the combination of the two is never really going to appeal. I ask all the other lads, and surprisingly they also pass. Herne Bay thinks we're all mental.

We leave the hotel at the same time as a group of German tourists. They look at us as if we have just escaped from the zoo and make no attempt whatsoever to disguise their amusement at this freak show. 'You typical English hooligans, ya?' Their interest prompts an 'Invaded Poland lately?' retort from one of the lads as we return their stares.

The sun is already hot as we make our way back down the same main drag that provided us with last night's 'entertainment'. Even at this early hour we encounter groups of Tunisian fans making their way up to the ground. Most are in good voice with drums, whistles and hooters adding to their noise. I can't help thinking that with over four hours to kick-off they might just burn themselves out. We pass by the same bar that witnessed last night's violence. In the bright light of a new day the place is now calm, although the smashed windows and piles of broken chairs bear testament to the events of the night before.

We turn the corner and start to head off towards the main port. Suddenly every ten yards we come across someone asking for tickets – not a good sign. On the front we find a line of bars. A large group of Tunisians occupies one area while a larger group of English supporters, all in good voice themselves, have taken up residence next door. A few yards away sitting on some railing I spot another group of English. These lads are quiet, their eyes fixed on the two groups, waiting, watching. Not one is wearing national colours. As we pass, Mr B also points them out and we agree that very soon something is likely to kick off.

As our priority is finding tickets we leave the situation behind and hunt down the American ticket agency. Pretty soon we stumble across the Irish bar and go to make our way in. From nowhere appears a very large Frenchman who proceeds to block our path. I ask him if the bar is open, but he just shakes his head and tells us to go. Inside I can see more of the same, all eyes fixed on us, and I begin to wonder if we have come across something we shouldn't have. Suddenly a man comes over whom I recognise as the owner of the bar. He is the man who was shown on breakfast TV back home, the one who told the world that you could get tickets for any England match. For a split second I think of asking him whether or not he has any spares, but he soon tells us that the bar has been shut and ushers us away.

We wander aimlessly around in the vain hope of stumbling across the ticket agency, but have no luck, so we stop for a swift half. The bar lady tells us that she doesn't know of any such agency, and it appears that we have been chasing a red herring.

On finishing our beers we head back to the bars on the front. The situation is pretty much as we had left it, but I soon hear one bloke talking about things kicking off any moment. To avoid getting caught up we cross the road and sit on the roundabout. Within minutes, things turn nasty.

There are certain things that separate many English football supporters from their foreign cousins, one of which is a complete lack of tolerance towards any other country's fans showing patriotism. We all know that the English are loud, very loud, but whereas the English will sing their hearts out, many continentals like to gesticulate, blow horns and generally be a pain in the arse by running up and down while waving flags in your face. As much as it hurts me to say it, I have to state that if flag waving and being a pain in the arse were an Olympic sport then the Tunisians would surely be battling it out with the Italians and Argies for the top spot. It was gestures such as these that finally brought things to a head.

As we looked on, one Tunisian lad pushed his luck that little bit too far as he rode his bike right in among the English supporters while waving his flag and generally giving it the large one. Pretty soon he found himself relieved of his vehicle, followed by a swift boot up the jacksy. As he made off some idiot threw a bottle at him, which prompted another ten or so like-minded idiots into doing the same thing. The Tunisians in the adjoining bar quickly ran for cover fearing the worst, but thankfully the majority of the English lads followed up their actions with a bout of singing rather than chasing after them. With the Tunisians making their exit I soon managed to pick out some of the faces that had attacked the bar we had been drinking in the night before, including the fat lad who had been leading their charge.

While this was going on the police seemed totally unprepared and just stood by as if waiting for someone to come along and tell them what to do. The whole incident was over in a matter of seconds, but once again it proved that wherever the two groups of fans mixed trouble was always likely to flare up.

As calm descended Mr B shouted at me to watch out. I turned round just in time to see a small lad, no more than eleven or twelve, throw a beer bottle at me from about ten yards away. Standing right by my side were four coppers. I managed to avoid the missile and waited for the Old Bill to grab the lad and give him a stiff cuff around the ear, but they just stood still and did nothing. A few other lads shouted at the coppers as the young Tunisian just stayed put, but the best they could do was gesture to the lad to piss off. The bottle thrower greeted their request by giving them the finger, then turned round and walked off while still looking over his shoulder and giving it large. You had to laugh, but it sort of hinted that the police were more interested in the English than the locals.

Not knowing what would happen next we quickly decided to move off in the direction of the ground. For all we knew the riot police could well have been heading our way at that very moment, teargas at the ready, and we still had tickets to track down.

As we got closer to the stadium the crowds grew bigger. By now we were all starting to get worried as we hadn't yet come across anyone with tickets to sell. Tunisian fans were busy riding up and down the main drag in their cars and on motorbikes, making as much noise as possible, while the English just looked on as they drank in the street cafés and bars that lined the route. The closer to the ground we got the greater the number of English fans, until they totally outnumbered the Tunisians and the scene turned into a wash of red, white and blue. It was obvious that the number of fans without tickets was vast and yet all were still hopeful as the singing grew constant and louder.

A small group of French riot police moved in to push back one group of England fans as they threatened to spill into the road, thus blocking the way through for the traffic. Their actions were met with a chorus of, 'If it wasn't for the English you'd be Krauts', a song that, although very funny at the time, was never going to help win the local bobbies over. The riot police were then joined by more officers in plain clothes, although the bright orange armbands they were all wearing did give their little game away somewhat.

Over the last ten years many things have happened to football that, in my opinion, have seen our great game take a turn for the worse. One such problem for me is the growth in the amount of people who think it's funny to dress up like a cunt whenever they intend going near a football stadium. Of course, I blame the Dutch for inventing this kind of behaviour, which I can only imagine has stemmed from their rather lax drug laws, but unfortunately this disease spread and now, thanks to the Channel Tunnel, has reached epidemic proportions on our side of the water.

One group of lads walks by dressed like the Knights of the Round Table, which I can kind of understand what with King Arthur and all that bollocks, but when a couple cross my path dressed as Superman and Wonder-Woman I have to physically restrain myself while asking the Lord above why he allows these people to walk his Earth. OK, so the man upstairs must have a sense of humour, but he has already given us the Spanish, so why this? Do these people honestly think that by dressing up in such a manner the camera crews will pick them out and beam their little joke into the living rooms of the world so that Hans, Mustafa and Gregori can go, 'Oh, those crazy English'? If so, they must also realise that many right-minded people are pointing at the screen and saying, 'Oh look. A wanker.'

As we make our way among the crowd Gary spots his mates from Gillingham and introduces me for the first time to their friend and our new room-mate, Tony. He looks about seven feet tall, is built like a rake and never looks you in the eye when he is talking to you, something I find very aggravating. He also has a very, very loud voice.

The search for tickets continues endlessly and becomes more desperate as the minutes fly by. I keep asking myself why I turned down the corporate ticket I had been offered earlier, and begin mentally to kick myself. It soon becomes apparent that the majority of the tickets up for grabs are in the hands of either the French, who have no interest in the game whatsoever and their one ticket to sell, or the local Arabs, who have tickets by the handful and are out to make as much cash as possible. Unfortunately for us, the asking price has stuck at around £100 due to people starting to panic. Like us, many decide on waiting until the last possible moment in the hope of picking up a ticket on the cheap, while others are talking of steaming the gates.

One lad next to me suddenly strikes up conversation with a Frenchman in his fifties who has one ticket to sell. The local is obviously not short of a few bob. He is well dressed and doesn't look the type to be touting a ticket outside a football stadium. He has with him a lady, whom I presume to be his wife, and another couple of around the same age, and for them this looks like an afternoon out rather than a football-watching day. Like everyone else this Frenchman is asking £100 for the ticket, so the lad hoping to take it off his hands does the sensible thing and checks that it is the real McCoy. To his surprise the ticket has no watermark, so he shoves it back in the palm of the Frog while also giving out a large dose of verbal. The Frenchman looks as surprised as everyone else gathered around, and busily checks the ticket himself. The four of them then take it in turns to hold the ticket skywards as they enter into heated discussion. I must admit, he doesn't look the type to be palming off dodgy tickets, but as the English dish out more verbal he and his friends quickly decide to make a rather swift exit.

The local Arabs are themselves much more organised and are moving around in groups openly selling their tickets while the police stand by and watch them go about their business. With so many English lads on the look-out I am amazed by the fact that not one ticket tout is getting turned over before having his tickets lifted. This may stem from the fact that more stories about people being stabbed the previous night are now doing the rounds, and people just don't fancy the risks involved in finding yourself in an argument with a local gang, no matter how small their numbers are. It soon gets to the stage where every person you pass is asking for tickets.

Then comes the moment when I think I've struck gold. As I shout my request for the thousandth time a lad next to me offers one up.

'I've got a ticket you can have cheap, mate.'

I can't believe my luck, and immediately another 20 lads crowd round.

'How much?'

'Well, I just paid 80 for it, but it ain't worth that.'

His answer completely throws me until his friend explains.

'Dozy twat just handed the money over without checking it first.'

'What is it, a dud then?'

'No, it's kosher. If you want to go and see Belgium play South Korea, that is.'

The lad had only realised his mistake after he had been turned away at the first checkpoint. The local who had sold him the ticket was now long gone.

By now the rest of the lads have decided that they would rather watch the game on the big screen set up down on the beach as the ticket prices have continued to stay high. Pretty soon, one final encounter with a tout persuades me to join them.

I spot a group of three lads who are busy being the centre of attention, so I head over in the hope of securing a late result. As I get to them I see lads turning away in disgust, but I take my chance.

'You selling?'

'Yes, pal.' Their distinctive accent instantly tells me they are from Merseyside. 'How many do you want?'

'Have you got four?'

'Yeah. Two hundred each.'

'Two hundred! Fuck off.'

'If you don't want them then you fuck off.'

Another lad who has joined the frenzy quickly voices his opinion. 'You thieving cunts. We're fucking English, mate. We should be looking out for each other not ripping our own off.'

The Scouser obviously doesn't share his patriotic stance. 'Tell you what pal, the beach is down that way.'

Honestly, I didn't believe that even a Scouser would try to rip his fellow countrymen off that badly. Why people continue to hold them up as cheeky little chaps with a great sense of humour is beyond me. I have travelled hundreds of miles in the hope of watching England kick off a game in the World Cup finals only to be finally ripped off by someone who calls himself a fellow Englishman.

With less than 15 minutes to go before kick-off I finally give up and head off in the direction of the beach. I later find out that not only have I missed out on seeing the match in the flesh, but also that back home you are treated to the sight of Jimmy Hill wearing a Cross of Saint George bow-tie. I really hope Sir Jim dressed just to offend Alan Hansen. I stroke my fingertips against the end of my chin in appreciation. Jim-meeee!

In every city playing host to World Cup matches the local authorities had set up large television screens so that all those without tickets could still get to watch the games while enjoying the next best thing to the atmosphere generated within the stadiums. As every step brought us closer to the arena the noise grew louder and the adrenalin began to flow. We soon heard a big cheer go up and a quick check of the watch told me that the game had finally started. The whole area in which the screen was situated had been fenced around, and before you were allowed in you had to go through some gates so that your bags could be checked. We soon learnt that due to the trouble of the previous few days the local authorities had sensibly placed an alcohol ban within the arena. Gary and Mr B decided to wait outside and watch from behind the fences rather than surrender their recently purchased refreshments, leaving Tony and I to go in alone.

The arena covered an area about the same size as four football pitches. The screen was large, positioned high enough up for everyone to get a clear view, and it gave off a fantastic image. Around the edge of the arena were catering vans and merchandising kiosks which all appeared to be doing good business, and at the back they provided a large temporary stand for spectators to sit in. Every seat in that stand appeared to be occupied by the local Tunisian population, and the first impression I got was one of being totally outnumbered. I soon also realised that there was no form of segregation whatsoever, so the alarm bells start to ring. I knew there and then that the second the ball hit the back of the net this would turn into a beach party with a very unhappy ending.

The noise the locals generated was both loud and annoying with screams, whistles and shrill cries piercing my eardrums. As the sun beat down I began to look around for some fellow Englishmen, but only managed to pick out the odd three lions shirt, but pretty soon my eyes fell upon a highly amusing sight. Standing by the side of the seating area I spotted a woman trying to keep her three children under control. All four of them were wearing England shirts; she was looking slightly harassed while the kids looked hot, bothered and thirsty. I couldn't help thinking that her old hubby must have life completely sussed. He took his wife and kids on holiday, then bunged her a few shekels before telling her to go and have a nice day out on the beach, while he buggered off to football. Pure genius. Surely if that man could bottle whatever it is he has that enables him to live such a heavenly lifestyle he would be a millionaire overnight.

Up on the big screen we could see the match was in full flow, and Paul Scholes very nearly put England a goal ahead. For the first time the Tunisians fell quiet, but their silence was short-lived as their whistles soon filled the air once more.

Within minutes Scholes missed an even better chance, and for the first time the cry of 'Ing-er-land!' could be heard from the area immediately in front of the screen, the English fans making their presence felt for the first time. The sudden outburst, although music to my ears, was taken rather differently by the Tunisians sitting in the stand. Within seconds a few stones and bottles were thrown in the direction of the English fans, and these were followed by a flare that left a bright orange trail as it flew towards its target. I looked around to assess the reaction of the security only to see a group of riot police stand by as if nothing had happened. Tony and I agreed it was only a matter of time, then Alan Shearer scored and the place went ballistic.

The second the ball hit the net the Tunisian fans fell silent. There is nothing better than seeing a load of mouthy bastards being shut the fuck up in an instant, and as they had been giving it the large one since we had entered the arena I was in pure heaven. I must admit that for me and nearly every other football fan I know, that is always a magic moment. However, the trickle of missiles they had been throwing since Scholes missed soon turned into a barrage, and all of a sudden we found ourselves right in the middle of what could only be described as a battle zone.

As the English gave it loads the Tunisian fans began to throw everything and anything they could get their hands on into the crowd in front of them. They threw ripped-out seats, stones and bottles, many of which landed on their own kind as well as England fans. Their actions caused panic as families tried to gather themselves together and people ran in all directions in order to find cover. A quick look over my shoulder also told me that the area where the police were once standing was now empty, the men in blue uniforms nowhere to be seen.

The England fans were forced back up against the big screen and fences from where there was no escape as the Tunisians continued to unload their never-ending supply of ammunition. Pretty soon an area of no man's land opened up between the two groups of supporters as the locals kept enough distance for them to throw their missiles but avoid getting caught up in hand-to-hand fighting. Up on the big screen you could see the players walking off for their half-time cup of PG, while here bottles and stones continued to land on the grass around my feet as I kept a keen eye on the direction of their origin.

To my right the main bulk of the England fans were gathered, and once the shower of danger had slowed down they made their move. As a large group of English steamed forward the Tunisians turned and legged it. As they went, the English supporters were screaming at the tops of their voices. Their charge prompted many of those trying to escape from the stand to run back up, and many began to scramble down the scaffolding at the side or climb over the back. One Tunisian fan, in his desperation to escape, slipped and fell some 20 feet to the ground. Once the English had cleared the area they stopped chasing after the locals and began to gather themselves once more. The momentary calm that followed enabled many to go back and collect any belongings they had left behind before making a hasty exit.

At this point I honestly felt that calm would be restored, but as the English regrouped under the big screen yet another group of Tunisian fans appeared throwing more missiles, only this time they came from the far side of the arena. The English fans were now well tooled up themselves, and once again they steamed off in the direction of the locals in order to give them a taste of their own medicine. This action was greeted by the sight of Tunisians once more doing the 100 metre dash. As the English ran at one group another mob of locals would appear from the opposite direction and start to unload their weapons.

Standing within the middle of the chaos I caught sight of something that will live with me for years. One lone England fan stood defiant as bottles flew around; he remained unmoved, beating out a rhythm on a snare drum. It always amazes me how people react in situations such as these, and the sight of the drummer only added to the unbelievable events that were unfolding before my eyes.

Suddenly I felt the dull thud of a stone hitting me directly in the knackers, so I thought it best that I try to make my way to a safer part of the arena. I looked around for Tony, but in the chaos we had already been split up.

As the dull thud of the stone turned into that familiar painful ache all men get when hit in the tender bits, I was passed by a black guy who was desperately shouting out for his mates. At first he seemed eager to get in on the action, but I soon realised that he was pointing towards a wound that had appeared just under his left armpit. I asked him whether he was OK or not, only to realise that he was in a mild state of shock and that the injury was in fact a stab wound. The poor bastard had just been plugged in the side by a Tunisian lad who ran past us. He didn't really know where he was, and the thought suddenly hit me that I could just as easily have been the one on the end of that blade. In the chaos I found it amazing that more people didn't get seriously injured, although the number of people walking by with head wounds and blood pouring down their faces was beginning to grow by the minute.

The mayhem continued between the two groups for what seemed like ages, before the cheer went up from the English to greet the arrival of a small group of riot police. At last I thought that order was about to be restored, but once again they stood motionless, appearing to wait for some kind of instruction. No more than ten yards in front of them was a group of Tunisians busy unloading their bottles and stones, yet they seemed powerless to act. Many of the Englishmen around me were calling out for them to do something, but even as their numbers grew the police stood by and watched the battle continue. On the far side another group of riot police appeared, so now they had the locals firmly situated between them, and there for the taking. We had been told so much about the French riot police on our televisions back home, yet when it came down to it and the shit hit the fan they didn't appear to have a fucking clue.

As we waited and waited for them to kick into action, what I assumed to be another flare landed about 20 yards from me. Pretty soon the smoke smothered me and entered my throat, and I began to gasp for air while finding it hard to breathe. As we had stood back and waited for the police to round up the Tunisians, one of their officers in charge had taken us all by surprise and ordered his men to fire teargas into the English fans instead. Soon we found ourselves under a shower of gas canisters. As the police fired at random, their actions caught not only those lads ready to mix it but innocent lads, women and children as well. The wind blowing off the Mediterranean only added to the stupidity of their actions as the choking gas was whipped around in all directions.

The police then moved forward, allowing the once-trapped Tunisians to go unchecked, and the local mob found itself behind the safety of the police lines, from where they continued to shower the English with whatever they could get their hands on. Thankfully, by this stage some England fans had managed to pull open a gap in the fences so that we could escape to the safety of a car park and fields situated behind the big screen.

The effects of the gas had now taken their full toll. As if getting air into my lungs wasn't hard enough, my skin had now begun to itch. The irresistible desire to rub my watering eyes soon gave them an added stinging sensation, until thankfully someone handed me a bottle of water with which to splash my face. All around me people of all ages were suffering in the same way as a sense of disbelief mixed with anger at the police's actions began to spread.

In all my years I can honestly say that I have never seen such inept police tactics being deployed in order to restore some form of control; their actions only spread this particular situation over a larger area. I am not saying for one moment that the English fans were angels, because that simply was not the case. There were plenty of lads down on the beach that afternoon desperate to have it away with the locals. I saw plenty of English lads grabbing at anything they could get their hands on, and then happily firing bottles and stones back at the Tunisians. And there were plenty of lads running in all directions hoping, above all else, to stick a size nine up the arse of some local. But it also has to be said that there were plenty of people in among them who had just found themselves caught up in a situation from which there was no escape. The main bulk of the England fans had been under the cosh for approximately three minutes before they finally took it upon themselves to retaliate and chase into the Tunisian fans.

Three minutes is a very long time to have potentially fatal weapons flying around your head. Three minutes of chaos must seem like an eternity when your kids are screaming, panic-stricken by the violence that is happening all around them. And three minutes is a long time to wait for the authorities to come and defend the rights of people who have suddenly found themselves under attack. Let me make this clear: the violence that erupted down on the beach that afternoon was started by the Tunisians. When that ball hit the back of the net putting England 1–0 ahead it was the Tunisians who started throwing their bottles, not the English supporters – we were too busy celebrating. The failure of the French police to protect those that had come under attack finally forced many of those people into defending themselves.

There were plenty of film crews taking footage that would clearly show the English fans chasing the Tunisians out before stopping and moving back towards the big screen into what they felt was a safe area. It is plain to me that those fans didn't continue after the Tunisians. They didn't trap them up against the fences in order to smash their heads. I never saw anyone run up into the stand to beat the crap out of those locals who still found themselves trapped. What the majority of those England fans did was to clear the area and then move back and wait for the police to finally make an appearance and restore calm. I have no doubt in my mind that that was the intention of most of those lads, and that was what I was witnessing down on the beach.

I have seen so much of this in my lifetime. Every time it happens you think the same thing. *This time they can't lie. This time they have to tell it like it was*. But deep down you know that will never happen. It is very easy for people to sit at home in their armchairs or in the Houses of Parliament and slag people off. It is very easy to stand back from, disown and pass judgement on people when you are hundreds of miles away. It is very easy to believe the loaded comments of people trying to pass the buck on television, or the journalist desperate for that sensational headline, but unless you are there and witness the events with your very own eyes, you only get a small slice of the true story.

It is impossible to understand the range of emotions that pass through the mind when you find yourself in situations such as these unless you are actually there surrounded by the noise, the heat, the smell and the chaos. You feel frightened, excited, angry and on edge. Your whole body is alive, buzzing as your brain tries to cope with all the messages your senses are picking up. It is also very hard to control those emotions. People will sit back and say you should just walk away and not get involved, which is easy when you're in the safety of a studio or your front room. But the reality of being there is something quite different. You can't help but be affected by what is happening. Some people will panic, while thankfully others will do their best to protect those around them when no one else will. Personally I've no idea how I would have reacted if I could have got hold of the Tunisian lad who had stabbed that black guy. Being perfectly honest, I imagine I would have tried to beat the shit out of him, whereas at any other time I would more likely have run a mile. People react to the circumstances in which they find themselves, and for those passing judgement back in Westminster they should take that into account before opening their often ill-informed mouths.

As I milled around the car park the sense of anger continued to grow. From the direction of the main exit police sirens rang out and I could see people running in all directions as the violence continued. My first thought was of Gary and Mr B; then the image of that woman wearing her England kit along with her three children shot into my mind. God only knows what happened to them; they were right in the firing line when everything kicked off. I only hope someone managed to get them to safety.

Many England fans had decided that they had seen enough and were now heading off across the field behind the big screen in the direction of the city port. Suddenly a loud shout went up and I turned to see yet another group of Tunisian fans appear from inside the arena area. Once again they aimed a barrage of missiles in the direction of people heading away, wanting to leave this whole situation behind. The sight brought the anger felt by so many England fans to a head once again, and very quickly a hundred or so lads steamed off in the direction of the locals, who soon turned and headed back. As the English fans chased in after them the air was suddenly full of the sound of more teargas canisters being fired. As the smoke rose it was clear that the English fans had become the target for the police, and this despite the fact that those local lads, so up for it just moments earlier, must have run directly past them!

Standing next to me I noticed a very old French gentleman. I looked at him and he just shrugged his shoulders. I couldn't help but apologise – my apologies to do with being a supporter of a sport that had come to his city and caused so much trouble. I wasn't going to apologise for being English.

Five more minutes passed before calm finally appeared to descend. The last I had heard England were 1–0 up, but a quick check of the watch told me that the second half was now well underway and so, like everyone else, I needed to find out what was going on up at the ground. Slowly, I made my way back to where the fences had been pulled open, only to be told by an officer of the law that the arena was now closed. By a small television van I could see a female reporter interviewing five lads with blood splattered all over themselves. Great TV, I thought, but where was the medical help? I took one last look down towards the main entrance, only to see the blue lights still flashing and people moving in all directions. It was time to move on.

My experiences were one thing, but what people had witnessed outside was something else. Davy, Essex WHU, tells all:

From where we were you could just about see the screen enough to realise Shearer had scored. We started cheering, of course, and it wasn't too bad at first, then people started running out of the field totally shitting themselves. We couldn't really see what was going on, or the stand that had all the fans in, but when people started climbing over the back you knew things were getting bad. The police outside with us looked like they never had a clue, and then a mass of Tunisian fans came running out and we guessed they must have been done by all the England lads. They were well fucked off, and pretty soon they started throwing bottles and attacking anyone who had an England shirt on. Me and the lads I was with thought, fuck this, we better get away, as it started to get well naughty. There was no way you could have a go back as they would have killed you.

I took my shirt off straight away and tucked it into my strides as best I could. That was horrible, that; I've never had to take my colours off before, ever, not in over ten years of going to football. But it was dangerous. Once they got hold of someone they were on them like dogs, loads of them. There was one lad we saw as we went by the roundabout who was well fucked. Not moving, nothing, and the coppers were trying to clear some space for the medics to get at him.

It's a dodgy one, being in situations like this. If you run you attract attention, if you try and walk you can get caught up – you don't know what to do. We headed back up the main road towards the ground and you had to have eyes in the back of your head. There were more of them coming down towards the beach so you had to get yourself through that as well. Any car with an English plate was getting trashed, and then we saw this bust-up between two birds that was amazing. This French or Tunisian girl, I couldn't tell, just started booting this car, and straight away this English girl jumped out and went loopy. At first she grabbed her by the hair and started whacking her. That then turned into a right cat fight before all these other Tunisians turned up and started kicking the car as well. This poor English bird didn't know where to go next. They mullered the motor, put the back window through and just about dented every panel there was, but again there was fuck all you could do to help 'cause they would have turned on you. It was really bad, very scary, with people getting lumped left, right and centre. God knows how we all managed to get away without getting a slap. The coppers were shit, although I don't know what they could have done anyway. They were well outnumbered and it was going off all over the place. Most of them were just kids, nasty little bastards.

When we got up by the ground it was a bit different. Some English lads had managed to get it together and were up for a pop back at them, but they just fucked off back to where they were on top. There was more Old Bill up at the ground as well, which made it safer. But a load of the English fans were giving them some real verbal for not getting in there and sorting it out. We just headed off back towards the centre and found a bar on the way down. There was no point in staying around there as it just looked like getting worse.

I had seen enough too, and decided to head off and find a bar in the hope of catching the last 20 minutes of the game. After walking no more than 100 yards I came across a French guy who had just been hit above the eye, blood pouring down his face. He was being comforted by a group of girls, and ten yards further on I could see the lad that had just hit him being restrained by his mates. What had sparked it off I don't know, but once again it proved that the relative calm could be shattered in the blink of an eye, and now that I was on my own I felt more than a little worried. Not least by the fact that I didn't actually know where the fuck I was.

Pretty soon I managed to find a bar that was crammed with England fans, and I settled myself down. I took a long look round and picked out many faces that I recognised from down on the beach. It was amazing to think that no more than twenty minutes ago these very same people had found themselves smack bang in the middle of a full-scale riot, and yet here they were enjoying a beer and acting as if nothing unusual had happened to them. Maybe I just have a happier home life than most, I don't know, but their desire to watch their national football team in action was all that mattered.

As Shearer and co. battled out the final stages on the pitch we put all that had happened behind us and got behind the team. In the final minute our support was rewarded as Paul Scholes more than made up for his earlier misses by unleashing an unstoppable shot into the back of the net. As the England team clinched three vital points the bar erupted and the world in which I live became a much happier place to be as all my worries disappeared to the back of my mind.

Sitting next to me were two young lads from Canada. I had to ask them what they had made of it all, and I have to say that their initial reaction surprised me. They told me how they had joined the England fans in chasing off the Tunisians whenever they steamed forward. They had wanted to see the English beat the shit out of the locals, and I had no doubt they were telling the truth after one of them explained what had happened to them the previous night:

We had gone out on the drink and had a really good night out. We stayed away from the port because we had seen what went on during the day and didn't want to get caught up in that again, so we drank in some of the smaller bars. Every one of them had football fans in and we met some great people. We did get really pissed, I must admit, and we stayed in one bar till about 3.00 a.m.

drinking with some locals who seemed really all right.

It got so late that we decided to go find a taxi, and left. We had only just got around the corner when this bloke from the bar came up and said he'd give us a lift to where we were staying, and you know what it's like when you're pissed, you just go with it. We got in the car and he drove off real slow. Then we stopped at this corner and all of a sudden another four blokes piled in and started beating the hell out of us, then they stole our wallets. The driver drove us to Christ knows where and they kicked us out. We ended up walking for a while, because for all we knew we could have been in a real bad part of the city. Then we just found an alley and waited down there until it got light. We didn't get back to the hotel until gone half past six. We didn't lose that much really as we had already drank most of the money we had on us, but I tell you, there is no way we are leaving this city without giving some Arab shit a good hiding.

The lump on the side of his head seemed to fit in with the story quite nicely, and considering what had happened to them they appeared to be in surprisingly good spirits, but stories like this always scare me. It's not that I am worried for my own safety, but rather that of the person passing their experience on. I mean, how many sandwiches short of a picnic do you need to be before accepting a lift at three in the morning from an Arab you don't even know, while wandering the streets of Marseille suddenly becomes a good idea? What a couple of tossers. We all have moments of madness in our lives – I even bought a David Essex single once – but their particular tale took the art of being a fuckwit to a whole new level.

After 15 more minutes the bar began to empty, and the time had come for me once again to brave the streets of Marseille. I only had a vague idea of what direction I should be heading in, and so the butterflies rose once more as I gingerly made my way through the very expensive-looking back streets. A few yards in front of me were two lads, one of whom had an

English Cross of Saint George flag tied around his waist. Immediately my brain reminded me of the old saying 'safety in numbers', so I took a short jog and struck up a conversation. Just like me, they didn't have a clue as to where they were, so each crossroads we arrived at had us voting on which direction was the best to take. The two lads were both from the People's Republic of Yorkshire and followed Leeds United, and we spoke excitedly about what we had seen in the hope that talk would help cure our anxiety.

Finally we worked our way through the maze of back streets and found ourselves at the end of a road that led up onto the main drag back to town. In the distance we could see the thousands of fans walking back towards the city centre, their leisurely pace suggesting that they were enjoying a walk unaffected by rampaging hooligans.

As one we breathed a sigh of relief and took the first few steps in the direction of safety, then suddenly some hundred yards ahead, and between us and the main street, a group of Tunisian lads came jogging into view. The looks they were firing over their shoulders suggested they were doing their best to get away from someone else, but unfortunately it was in our direction that they were heading. Quickly we turned and headed up a road that ran at right angles from the one we had wanted to travel on in the hope that we could avoid getting trapped.

This area of the city must have been one of the most wealthy as the houses and apartments looked magnificent. As we passed by a school all three of us broke into one of those 'I am not really scared and trying to get away without you noticing me' walks that most football supporters come to master during their time. The people wearing their designer clothes and waiting to pick up their children must have wondered what the hell was going on, but soon the mob came into view and started up the street after us. A quick glance over my shoulder confirmed to me that we had been spotted, and now a couple of their lads at the front had broken into a full-blown sprint. A gut-wrenching feeling that only occurs at such moments shot through my body as all of a sudden we found ourselves in a pretty dodgy situation.

Now, like most blokes, I don't like being run, but I also don't pretend to be some kind of hero ready to take on all comers. I had already seen one bloke stabbed today and I didn't fancy becoming the second. I already know my wife didn't marry me for my looks, but I don't need to make a poor job any worse, so it was time to do the off. I was quite pleased to see that even at the tender age of 34 I still had the running on the Leeds lads, and within seconds I was heading the race. It's amazing what your legs can do when your arse is about to give way. The Tunisian lad leading their charge soon found himself alone as his friends gave up the chase, and from somewhere deep down that overwhelming urge to give him a right-hander suddenly entered my mind. Maybe it was due to the fact that I had simply had enough of being run down side streets, or that now the odds were even I fancied my chances – I don't know, but I hate being run. It leaves an awful feeling in the pit of my stomach, as it does in most other blokes I know, and I would have loved to stick one on that lad, just one. He couldn't have been more than 18, no more than a kid, but in the back of my mind stories of people getting stabbed were still ringing the alarm.

Once again we found ourselves at a junction and swung a right which took the road back towards the main drag and safety. Just a few yards down from that junction and hidden from view we came across an entrance to a block of apartments, down which a woman was driving her car. As we scooted past she shot forward, just as the lad chasing after us appeared, and he went crashing into the side of her vehicle, halting him in his tracks. All three of us couldn't help but piss ourselves laughing. Dozy twat. Suddenly, all thoughts of confrontation disappeared from my mind, and as the rest of his mob came to pick him up we broke into a final little jog and made it to the safety of the main drag.

As I joined the throng of supporters making their way from the stadium, a feeling of relief swept over me. It was as if everything I had witnessed that afternoon shot through my mind in a matter of seconds, only to be quickly followed by the knowledge that I had managed to get through it all without suffering anything more than a slight pain in the groin. The people walking next to me must have thought I was off my chump as I walked down that road laughing happily to myself, but I didn't care – I was alive.

Within ten minutes I had said my farewells to the Leeds lads and was back in my hotel – and boy, was I happy to be back in that hotel. Sitting in the bar area were the rest of the lads who thankfully had also managed to get through the afternoon unscathed. We had been joined by Gary and Mr B's friends from Gillingham, and we soon began to swap stories surrounding the day's events. Whereas I had been ripped off, tear-gassed and run, their experiences had been slightly less traumatic.

The Gillingham fans had travelled down on the TGV overnight, arriving in Marseille during the early hours of the morning. As they were travelling back and forth for each England game they were prepared to pay whatever it took in order to purchase tickets, and so getting hold of them hadn't proved much of a problem. They had actually been approached by an American guy who had tickets by the fistful to sell. They couldn't believe how he had managed to get hold of so many when there were so many desperate English fans. At the time they thought his asking price of £120 each was a fair deal and so took him up on his offer and bought four. He told them to keep a look-out for him at the rest of the England games as he would be getting tickets for all of those fixtures as well. All of their tickets were stamped with one company's name.

One of the people in the group was a young lady called Sharon and she had obviously had a top day out, describing the atmosphere in the stadium as the ultimate buzz. Now they were just winding down, enjoying a few beers and killing time until they needed to head off back to the train station in order to catch the TGV back home. They hadn't had any hassle or seen any trouble. For them it had just been a fantastic match and an unforgettable trip. Lucky bastards!

As we sat around talking I quizzed Sharon about her love for the great game. In the past I have taken the odd dig at women who follow football, but this particular filly soon left me in no doubt about her feelings about the sport:

> I've been going to Gillingham for years. They're my local club and I would never have supported any other team. At school we had all the lads in their Liverpool and Arsenal kits, and they would take the piss out of us lot wearing a blue shirt, although we soon made them shut up. The thing is I know that they never went to see the team they say they supported, and still don't go today. You can still see the same lads walking around town in the latest shirt as though they are the greatest fans in the world, but they are not football fans. A football fan is someone who goes every week, home or away. I don't see the point in supporting a team you never get to see.
>
> One thing that really gets to me is when I see people at Priestfield supporting the Gills but wearing another team's shirt. I would rather they stayed at home listening to Radio 5 and wearing out the Ceefax button. They can stick the Premier League up their arse for all I care. There is no better feeling than turning a big side over. All that money and the greedy bastards still get beat every now and then, just like we did at Coventry.
>
> Following England is the business, there is nothing like it. We all stick together and help each other out. If someone hasn't got a ticket everyone will try to bunk them in. If someone is getting grief everyone else will help them out. I don't regret paying £120 for a ticket because watching England abroad is the ultimate, and after all this is the World Cup. It's a long way to come just to stand outside.

There is no doubt that Sharon is as passionate, loyal and

obsessive a football supporter as any person you could hope to meet. She knew more about the game than I could ever hope to store within my tiny head, and I am sure she could sing for just as long and with just as much passion as any bloke I have ever met. The problem that I have is that not every woman that goes to football is like Sharon, and at this stage I have to be honest: I thank the Lord that they are not.

I really like being a bloke. I like having a laugh with a mob of blokes, and I like doing blokey stuff. Moaning, swearing, farting, ranting. Man's stuff. As it turns out, most men's behaviour in the cold light of day is idiotic, highly stupid and very embarrassing. Fortunately for me, and many like-minded blokes, the football stadiums provide the perfect place in which to act in such a manner. Or at least they used to. There can be no doubt that football is a male-orientated sport. It's mainly played by blokes, watched mostly by blokes. There are people who will hit the roof at that opinion, but I couldn't give a toss, because I only have to open my eyes to confirm I am right. Go down any park on a Sunday and you'll see hundreds of blokes enjoying the game they love. Take a panoramic view of any football stadium on a match day and you will see many more blokes than women. It makes me angry that football panders to the minorities in order to widen its fan base, and that such pandering is done largely against the desires of the majority, which no matter what they try to do or say will always remain blokes. Blokes, blokes, blokes. Blokes everywhere. But only man-type blokes please. No girlie ones.

However, here I would like to point out that I am not one of those people who think that women have no part to play in the game. Obviously women have just as much right to enter any football stadium as I or any other bloke does – someone has to heat the pies up. But that shouldn't mean that the majority should change their habits. I do get pissed off when some lad brings his girlfriend along for the first time and then starts asking me to sit down, not to shout and to watch my language because his loved one may get offended. Every football ground in the country has in the past had traditional areas where the main bulk of support has been vocal lads. This is the part of the ground from where the real atmosphere is generated, and always has been. Slowly but surely these areas are being eroded by chief executives and administrators who have little or no sense of history. Some even have no traditional support for the club, just that it happens to be their current employers. As those people tighten their grip around the neck of the game, these special areas within our football stadiums have began to disappear, and the atmosphere along with them.

A football team is a focal point for a display of loyalty that cannot be found in any other walk of life. The bond between supporter and club is handed down from generation to generation and remains lifelong, and if the game wants to sell, sell, sell then those are the money shots. Tradition, loyalty and passion, not the half-time entertainment, plastic seats or the catering at the United burger bar.

The people in the game that are so desperate to appear politically correct should get into the real world and understand that, for the vast majority of their paying punters, going to football is like nothing else they can experience. For them going to football isn't an excursion for the family unit. It's not a day trip to the local swimming pool, or like taking the kids to the pictures. The football stadium is a place for letting off steam, a place to bond with people who share your passion and who share your dreams. If one member of the group finds the experience alien and fails to understand the emotions being shared by all those around them, then that person can have the effect of killing the thrill for everyone else. When that golden moment arrives and your centre forward hits the back of the net the feeling is electric. It's a feeling you want to share, a magical moment when you become united with your fellow believers. But that moment can be shattered, utterly shattered, by the sight of some sour face who doesn't understand. If you have just one non-believer, one person along for the ride who fails to grasp the bonding that is taking place among the people all around them, then their effect can be devastating for the rest. Yet there are still those that run football who fail to understand; people continue to seek them out as though they are the golden key to everlasting success. The reality is quite different, of course. For those types of people, going to football is seen as an occasional day out rather than a lifetime's obsession. They will always remain mere spectators rather than supporters, and if that special bond isn't there then pretty soon neither will they. My only worry is that they will have taken many more with them.

We sat in the hotel bar and watched Romania beat Colombia 1–0. The good news from England's point of view was that both teams looked shite, but in Romania the match provided a far more sinister reaction. Pavel Veber was so incensed at his wife when she switched the television over during the first half of the match that he beat her to death. Mr Veber was arrested by police moments later in his local pub while watching the second half!

As our hotel bar slowly began to fill up, we were soon joined by Colin from Gloucester, the guy who had offered me the corporate ticket earlier in the day. After being introduced to me by Herne Bay he started apologising for asking £100 for the ticket by saying, 'Sorry. I know it was over the odds, but it had to be worth a hundred, didn't it?' Well, no, not really. If you want to rip me off that's your choice, but please don't apologise while you're doing it. You're either on the make or you're not, matey. The ticket was worth the face value as I saw it, which happened to be just £30. I had already shelled out over £250 on this trip and didn't really like getting ripped off by a fellow Englishman who then tried to make himself feel better with a poor excuse for being a money-grabbing arsehole.

There are many people who would gladly have paid that price, especially after travelling all that way, but as I said at the time, there was that little nagging voice in my head that told me to pass it up. Pretty soon I found out that I was right to follow my instincts, as Colin told me what had happened:

I ended up selling the ticket to this lad from Birmingham for £100, but it turned out to be a nightmare. I didn't just want to sell the ticket to anyone because I was going to have to sit next to them at the game and I didn't want to end up sitting next to some meat-head, so I hung on to it until I got drinking and talking to a few blokes who I thought were OK before letting them know I had a spare. This lad and his mates were all right and I had a good laugh with them. I sold him the ticket and we carried on drinking until just over an hour before kick-off, then we all walked to the ground together. It made sense to stay with him because we were sitting next to each other.

He was all right this bloke, just your typical England fan. I must admit he did look a bit of a handful – cropped hair, shirt off, a Cross of Saint George hanging round his neck – but so what? There's nothing wrong with that. We had a good old sing-song at the bar with everyone else, and the lad I sold the ticket to had an air horn which helped start most of the singing.

We decided to leave the bar about an hour before kick-off, and once we got up there his mates went their separate ways and we went off to our section. Getting through the first couple of check points was no problem, but once we got to our section it all kicked off. I've gone through first, no problem, but as he went to go through after me this copper stopped him and just said no, he weren't going in. I am standing there wondering what the hell is going on, then I see him showing the ticket to another bloke and he is obviously getting a bit worried about getting in. It didn't matter what he said, the policeman was still not having it, and pretty soon more police gathered round him. One policeman takes the air horn off him, then they start unwrapping the flag and just giving him a hard time. There was no reason for it. He wasn't drunk, playing up or anything like that.

The lad from Birmingham suddenly realised he might not get in and started shouting to me to come back and tell them he was with me. But as soon as he started shouting this other policeman cracked him on the side of the head with his truncheon and he went down. Then the rest of them were on him like a shot. It was totally unjustified and out of order. He was shouting his head off and putting up a right old fight and all this happened right outside the hospitality bit with everyone looking on. They quickly had him handcuffed, and then kept him pinned up against the railings for a few minutes and were being really heavy-handed with him, kicking and punching. In the end it took about ten of them to carry him off. I felt terrible, but there was nothing I could do about it. He probably now thinks I sold him a dodgy ticket or something.

It was mad; one minute we were just about to go in and enjoy the game together, the next that happened. I think the police just took one look at him and thought, no way, he isn't getting in here. What kind of police are they to do that? Maybe because it was hospitality or something I don't know, but when I got inside there were plenty of other lads with England shirts on and flags. He's probably been deported now or something.

As we sat around, stories started to circulate that the local police had put on a special train in order to get as many English out of the city as possible. According to the rumours, the train was departing the main station late that night and heading straight for Calais, so Herne Bay headed off to the room and began to pack his bags. At this stage the temptation was certainly there for joining him, but as the room was already booked I thought better of it, so a final night out on the streets of Marseille was soon planned.

Once again we found ourselves at the bar opposite the local Old Bill station, only this time the police had blocked off the road to traffic and were telling us that it was not wise to go any further as the locals were out for more trouble. They went on to explain to us that the port area had been closed off as it was not safe for England fans, that the best thing we could do was go back and drink in our hotel. On hearing this I was more than happy to follow their instructions, but as ever Mr B and Gary fancied taking a little walk 'just to see for themselves', whether the Old Bill were telling the truth or not. Personally I believed them; I wanted to believe them as I'd had enough already.

As I sat in the bar talking to a group of lads from Liverpool (well, I'd have been on my own otherwise), small groups of local lads walked past at various times, obviously scouting the bars for England fans and the possibility of more trouble. Gary soon returned without anything to report while Mr B couldn't make out why no one was selling drugs on the street corners 'in this of all cities'. Having to keep an eye on the street at all times soon became too much of a pain, so the second the whistle went to signal the end of Germany's 2–0 win over the USA we decided that Marseille had little else to offer and made our way back to the hotel in order to get some much-needed kip.

The German team had suffered some terrible press back home in the build-up to this tournament: players too old, no inventiveness in their play, all that kind of stuff. And so some had taken it upon themselves to install television sets in over 300 churches so that they could watch the match and pray at the same time! I can't help thinking that somehow the prayer 'Please Lord, help Jurgen cheat his way to another penalty' seems a little misguided.

Back in the room we flicked through the television channels hoping to catch some news reports, and soon became aware that the English fans were mainly being held to blame for the trouble that had erupted that day. Deep down we all should have realised that things were never going to be any different.

Oh, I Do Like to be Beside the Seaside!
Day 7: Tuesday, 16 June

Today we rose early, settled up at the hotel and quickly made our way down to the train station in order to get away from the shite hole that is Marseille as soon as we possibly could.

As we sat on the vast bank of steps that led up to the main entrance of the terminal the sun shone down brightly and the city suddenly took on a completely different feel. From our new vantage point Marseille, this city on the Mediterranean, looked stunning as we gazed out upon the beautiful buildings, tree-lined roads, romantic port area and, of course, the beautiful deep-blue sea. What a shame it happens to be the home of so many bastards.

The general feeling among all the England fans hanging around was that they couldn't wait to get away. There were many more stories doing the rounds of people getting stabbed and that over 40 English fans had ended up in hospital. It was said that one guy had had his throat slashed, while another was in a serious way in hospital after taking a terrible beating in which he suffered a ruptured spleen. There were also many rumours about the British police picking out known faces for the local Old Bill to tug and ship back home at the first available opportunity.

Our main problem at this stage was deciding on where to go. At first we had chosen Toulouse, the venue for England's next game, so that we could start hunting out a match ticket before the main bulk of the England fans arrived. Then, after a short discussion with two lads from Manchester, we decided that France was no longer for us and that Barcelona seemed a much more exciting option. This would be followed by a few days on the beach having the large one at Lorett, just up the Spanish coast. As the indecision continued, we boarded the train, flicked a coin and, to the total dismay of Tony, ended up opting for Toulouse once again.

As the TGV headed west we soon began to share stories with our fellow travellers, and it was on this journey that we first struck up conversation with Wiltshire, although it wasn't the first time I had seen him on this trip. He had made himself known to me on the very first night when the bar we were in had come under attack. I had just started to take some pictures of the violence when he approached me and asked me to stop. When I tried to explain that it was all right for me to take pictures as I was English, he cut me short, told me that he didn't give a fuck where I was from and threatened to stick the camera up my arse if I continued. At the time I quickly considered the aggressive yet thoughtful manner with which he had placed his request and decided to heed his advice and thank him for his trouble.

We soon found out that, like many of the England fans out in France, he was travelling alone due to a cock-up with the ticket allocation, but he followed England wherever and whenever he could. Pretty soon I asked him if he would like to make up the numbers by joining us. It quickly became apparent that he was a known face among the England fans, and he certainly knew his stuff when it came to football. As we talked about the events we had both witnessed at the bar two nights before, I soon realised that, like so many England fans, he was more than prepared to stand and slug it out if the going got tough. As far as Wiltshire was concerned, when you travel with England you are on duty from the moment you wake up, something I was getting used to hearing. You didn't necessarily go looking for it, but if it came your way you never turned your back. For him and many others that was a major part of following your country – being proud to defend the fact you were English. The conversation we had had outside that bar two nights earlier had left me in no doubt that those were indeed his firm beliefs.

Wiltshire is only a small bloke. Not that well built, quiet and often thoughtful. Over the next seven days I was also to find out that he was intelligent, a chancer and a bloody good laugh. At the moment he was unemployed, and as far as the local DSS was concerned he was walking the Lake District trying to find himself. I was sure that at this stage he was gauging my reaction and was highly suspicious as to just who I was and what I was up to. I am fully aware that people who stand around on the edge of things with cameras are often not who they pretend to be. I know that people such as Wiltshire have every reason for not wanting to have their photographs taken, as they often find themselves placed on the NCIS register at New Scotland Yard and branded for life, whether they were involved in the incident or not. For the record, I am also fully aware that my name is currently being held on more than one register at that wonderful institution, despite the fact that I have no criminal convictions. So I fully understood where Wiltshire's anxiety was coming from.

Our conversation was suddenly broken by a lad who insisted on placing a can of lager into my hand. He was wearing a Sunderland shirt and his size suggested that it was indeed he who ate all the pies. He quickly began to explain his actions. 'There, that's for you, lad. Thanks to your lot [Watford] winning at Fulham on the last Sunday of the season, I won over six grand.' Six thousand pounds, and all I got was one can of lager, and a small one at that! And there was me thinking pies were cheap up north. He went on to explain that he had placed an accumulator bet at the start of the season on Arsenal, Notts Forest, Notts County and, of course, the Hornets winning their respective divisions. He had been sweating on our result coming in because as we went into the last game of the season Bristol City were top of the league and favourites to win the title. On that Sunday, by some quirk of fate he had found himself in Bristol when the results came through, and come 4.45 p.m. he was celebrating just as much as any Rovers fan the fact that Bristol City had fucked up at Preston. It was thanks to that winning bet that he was here in France with the rest of his mates, pissing it up on the TGV. He went on to tell us that the press back in England were slaughtering the English fans, and that a friend of theirs who had told his wife that he was off visiting his parents for the weekend had had his photograph printed on the front page of the *Daily Mirror*, much to the surprise of his missus.

The train was packed with football supporters from all over the world, and along the way I met two New Zealanders and two Canadians who said that getting tickets back in their home countries hadn't been a problem as their national teams had failed to qualify. The ticket shambles was highlighted once again, as all four lads told me that they had been to the England game while many of us Englishmen had been pointed in the direction of the beach. Bloody disgraceful.

Two solid hours of drinking followed before the train finally pulled into Montpellier station and I realised that all of us had made the journey without having our tickets clipped, giving me an extra day's rail travel free – result. As the train began to slow down many England fans began to get their things together and started to inform us that this city was close to the beach and had a student population of over 80,000! Sod Toulouse.

While in the queue at the tourist information office, I began talking to two English lads who had been put through a rather worrying few hours back in Marseille the previous night. They told me that their hotel had cocked things up and had failed to book them their room for the third night running, so on the evening of the game they had found themselves with nowhere to stay. They had met up with a few of their mates who were more than happy to let them bunk into their place, but on inspecting the room these two had decided that having four sleeping on the floor of a dingy back room was already a couple too many, and had just left their luggage for safety before chancing their luck and looking for something else.

Fortunately for them they had soon got chatting to two French guys who seemed really concerned about their predicament and did all they could to try to find them a room by making phone calls on their behalf. In the end, and when all the options had run out, these two guys generously said that the two English lads could crash out at their place rather than risk sleeping on the streets. Our two heroes couldn't believe their luck. The four of them had got on so well that the two French guys had offered to buy them a meal before they travelled off home, the English lads offering to return their hospitality if ever the two garlic munchers came over to England.

Everything was going swimmingly until the hosts announced that they were indeed a gay couple, listing their hobbies as working out and oiling each other up on the beach. The final nail in the coffin came when one of these happy chappies told them that he was a karate expert, wanted to travel the world and loved small furry animals. And there was me thinking that being down on the beach with the Tunisians was dangerous! These poor lads had inadvertently lined themselves up for a different kind of stabbing altogether.

As the food became less appetising they had decided that their only option was to do a runner, so under the pretence of going to powder their noses they had made their escape through a side door and remained intact, as it were. They had then run all the way back to their friends' room without looking over their shoulders, and on arrival had to bribe the doorman in order to get inside. I could see that even telling the story brought them out in a cold sweat, while the rest of us had tears rolling down our cheeks.

On arriving at the front of the queue we were quickly told that all the hotels in Montpellier were fully booked with the Italians and Africans already firmly entrenched, so we ended up having to travel out of the city to the small coastal town of Palavas, along with every other Englishman that had arrived that afternoon. As it turned out this place was a godsend following the complete chaos of Marseille. It was quiet, had a lovely beach, plenty of boats, loads of bars and, more importantly, there were no filthy little locals with blades running around.

Once we arrived at the Hotel Tanagra Tony quickly got the hump once more as Mr B, Gary and I took one room while he was shunted off to share with Wiltshire and another guy we had picked up called Barry. Following a few questions the owner of the hotel soon told us that he could get match tickets for the Italy v. Cameroon game the following day for £40. He went on to tell us that there was a bar around the corner from where we might well be able to obtain tickets for the England v. Romania game. A quick shower followed, then we were off to the bar, just in time to watch Scotland play Norway. Unfortunately we soon found out that just about every other England fan in the town had also been tipped off, which had me suspecting that this was some kind of sham just to attract more punters. Clever sods.

The table next to us was occupied by three England fans from Portsmouth: a young lad in his early twenties, a very attractive woman in her mid-forties and a blind guy of around the same age. I asked him what it was like for blind spectators at football, and what his experiences of France '98 had been like so far, considering all that had been taking place:

I've been going to football since I was a kid. I've been lucky because I have always had people around me who were willing to look out for me and talk me through the game, so it's always been quite easy. The facilities at clubs throughout the country are obviously much better now than they used to be, but I never use them as I like to be in with the main bulk of supporters rather than shut up in a room listening to the radio commentary. As you can imagine, I get the most biased account possible. If Pompey are playing well, you would think they were the best team in the world ever if you listened to what my friends tell me. But when they play badly then it's the complete opposite, the pits of the earth. It's very hard for me to explain the differences because I don't know what it's like for you as I've always been blind, but I love the atmosphere and the banter that goes on and I wouldn't miss it for the world.

We've enjoyed it over here so far, although at times it's been a bit scary. We were down at the port when it all kicked off and it was very different to when something happens back home. At least in England ninety-nine times out of a hundred you can get out of the way or avoid trouble altogether; over here they don't seem to worry about who gets hit, tear-gassed or charged at. It's not just worrying for me but for the people looking after me as well. I am totally in their hands. Without them I am useless really, so they have to do their best to stay calm and look after me while all hell is breaking loose. It's really hard to keep your emotions in check when there are people running all over the place screaming and shouting. I can hear it in their voices if they are scared, which doesn't make it any easier for me. It's when you hear bottles smashing right next to you and people steaming past that it gets very scary. You're just waiting for something to hit you, and that's really horrible. Also, like everyone else we had been told that the local kids were stabbing England fans, and let's face it, you are not going to get many easier targets than me, are you? But for all that we got out of there without a scratch so I am not complaining, and I must say that the French people have been great to us wherever we've been, really helpful.

As far as getting tickets for the England games goes, we've had no luck. We are not members of the travel club. It's pointless for someone in my situation as I want to be in with everyone else rather than be treated like some kind of sad case. Can you imagine what our chances are of getting three tickets together? Not a chance in hell. We don't go to that many England games to make it worth our while, so we would never clock up enough points to get one anyway. It's a total waste of time. If you've got the money you can get a ticket for anything, everyone knows that. But if you're just an average person like us then they'll walk all over you until someone else comes along who has deeper pockets. The way this tournament has been run is a total joke, it almost makes the people that run the game back home look like experts. The organisation here has been useless.

After watching the Scots scrape a 1–1 draw against a dismal Norway team we began to console ourselves with the fact that the sweaties, having given themselves a lifeline, are bound to trip up on it, lose to Morocco and fail to qualify.

Gary, Mr B and myself soon found ourselves with a bad case of the munchies, so we left the Pompey fans with the rest of the lads and went off in search of something to eat. Up in Bordeaux one group of Scottish fans had already seen to their stomachs by paying £1,400 to have ten curries specially prepared and flown over to them from their favourite curry house in Bournemouth. Two crates of lager were also added to the bill – there's a surprise.

The hours shot by as we moved from bar to bar and truly relaxed for the first time since arriving in France. Before we knew it we had watched Brazil slaughter Morocco 3–0, and the night had well and truly closed in on this sleepy little port.

Suddenly we realised that we hadn't seen hide nor hair of any of the other lads for hours, so off we went to track them down. Within minutes we came across Wiltshire and Barry, who had hooked up with an English lad who had settled in the town and knew everyone and his dog. The only person missing was Tony, whom Wiltshire presumed had been with us all night. The local lad, Dee, turned out to be an absolute diamond. He was one of those guys who has a permanent smile on his face, and he laughed at every opportunity. As we drank well into the early hours, he took us from bar to bar introducing us to the locals, and you were left in no doubt that he must have been the most popular bloke in the village. We soon learned that our local guide had been a bit of a tearaway in his youth, and this had resulted in him spending more than a few years in one of Her Majesty's Hotels. He explained that he had found himself in Palavas following his last stretch during which he had decided that the only way to put an end to it all was to leave England behind and start all over again. He had travelled virtually all over the world, but on his last trip the boat pulled into Palavas and he hadn't been anywhere else since.

While we told him all about Marseille, Mr B moaned about the difficulty he was having in obtaining drugs. However, his eyes soon lit up when our host informed him that if it was drugs Mr B wanted, then he had come to the right place. During the day Palavas was your typical sleepy holiday town, but by night the port area was busy with a different type of traffic altogether. Over the next few minutes Dee disappeared and there were various comings and goings, until finally Mr B ended up with a broad smile on his face and a rather iffy-smelling cigarette in his hand. Also doing the rounds was a very strange little substance that you rubbed directly onto your teeth. Apparently it made your head go bang for about 30 seconds. I decided that I'd rather stick to the lager.

We continued to prop up the bar while enjoying the very friendly hospitality of the portly French bar owner, until suddenly the whirlwind arrived and our evening out went totally tits up following the unexpected appearance of a rather unhappy Tony.

'Where the fuck have you lot been?' he said, shouting the words at the top of his voice. As everybody in this quiet little bar jumped out of their skin, the waitress moved towards him and asked him what was wrong. 'You can fuck off. I'm talking to them.' The anger in his voice made her jump, while the bar owner, who had been drinking out front with us, rose to his feet and calmly walked back behind his bar. Tony marched relentlessly forward, straight up to the bar, leant on it and started shouting at the rest of us. 'I want a drink. I ain't got no money, so someone get me a fucking drink. I've had nothing to eat either. I've been sitting in the room waiting for you lot all fucking night. You're fucking out of order, the lot of ya. Out of order.' He then faced the bar owner, who was now walking the length of the bar towards him, and shouted out his next demand: 'Get me a fucking lager.'

As the bar owner bent down, Dee suddenly lifted himself over the counter and grabbed at the bar owner's hands. The look on the owner's face was almost blank as he stared back at Tony, who remained totally oblivious to the scene he had caused. Dee turned to us and told us we should get Tony out quick. As the bar owner fixed this blank psychotic stare on Tony he was joined by the waitress who tried to calm him and give Dee time to get himself that side of the bar so that he could also have a calming word in his ear. As Gary and Mr B stood back looking embarrassed, the rest of us tried to talk some sense into Tony's head, his only reply being, 'Get me a fucking beer and I'll calm down.'

Dee kept gesturing to us to get Tony out, but he wasn't moving, and eventually the situation returned to some kind of normality. We were later to find out that the bar owner was rumoured locally to have been an armed robber and had not long ago come out after a ten-year stretch. This bar in Palavas was his nest egg, and the waitress his young girlie. Dee told us that Tony had chosen the worst place possible in which to act like a total prat. The bar owner was a lovely bloke who had, like him, learnt his lesson behind bars, yet he didn't suffer fools gladly. On seeing Tony's arrival and hearing his verbal attack on the waitress he had gone behind the bar in order to get at his shotgun to blow Tony's head off. It all sounded a bit far-fetched at first, until Dee reminded us of the blank look on the owner's face: 'Believe me, that's the look of a madman about to flip over the edge.'

As if the situation wasn't bad enough already, Tony then told us that the hotel owner had banned him and was not going to allow him back in. When asked why, Tony explained that he had broken the shower, then had a shouting match with the main man to cap it all off. It was unbelievable to think that all this was coming from a grown man in his late forties. On hearing this latest instalment from 'Tony's World' I couldn't help but think that if Dee had been in the toilet at the time of Tony's arrival, the bar owner may well have had enough time to have got to the gun, blown Tony's head off and saved us all a lot of grief. What a total arse wipe. The words 'You'll like Tony', spoken by Mr B and Gary two days earlier, came ringing back in my ears as they stood by not knowing where to put themselves.

For some reason I took it upon myself to go back to the hotel and smooth things over with the owner. He told me that Tony had been shouting at the top of his voice and waving his arms around, and that he didn't understand why my friend was acting in such a way in his hotel. I have to be honest and say that at times like these I feel ashamed of some of my fellow countrymen. The hotel owner had taken us in on good faith, which, it is worth remembering, wasn't in huge supply following on from the newspaper and television reports of Marseille, and Tony had shown him little or no respect in return. He was a nice bloke with a business to run and really didn't need twats like Tony coming into his establishment. Once I had convinced him to give the prat another chance, I couldn't leave before setting one thing straight with the owner: 'Please remember, that man is no friend of mine.'

Back home in England, the media outcry following the violence at Marseille had reached unbearable levels, with the government urging employers to consider sacking any of their workmen who found themselves convicted. As ever, knee-jerk reactions and comments such as these are ill-founded and unwise, as at this early stage not even a quarter of the truth had been exposed. Unfortunately, some never learn and take such suggestions on face value, and that can have devastating effects on the lives of many. A.L. from the south of England suffered more than most.

I had travelled down on my own on a coach run by a company up north and, being a member of the England Travel Club, I had tickets for the first four games. I only arrived in Marseille on the morning of the game, but within an hour I found myself well and truly tucked up. I had met a few decent lads on the coach and we went up to the ground together and hung out for a while with the rest of the England fans. When I got up there a large group of Tunisians was walking up and down the main road right by the stadium, and they were really baiting the English fans stood by on the pavement.

I was on the verge of crossing the road to go into the ground when the Tunisian lads came back up yet again, and this time there was a load of riot police behind them. Which seemed stupid really, as they would have been better off being between them and us. Then some of the Tunisians started giving the English the come-on to fight, and a few glasses got thrown. That started it off. There was no way I could cross the road because, like a load of others, I got caught under the bottle throwing. Standing next to me was this girl screaming her head off. She had been hit in the face by a brick or something and she was a right mess, blood and skin everywhere. A big gap opened up as the Tunisian fans ran back and I started shouting at the police to get someone over to help her out. The police just ran forward charging the English fans and hitting out at anyone they could catch. I saw this bloke next to me get hit and thought, that's it, I am off. As I turned to run I felt this smack on the head, and then I got jumped on by loads of plainclothes police. I couldn't believe it. One minute I am just about to go into the game, then I try to help this woman, then I am getting a hiding myself. They handcuffed me and I got dragged away and put in a car with two other blokes before being driven miles and taken to the cells.

At first I was just angry and pissed off at missing the game, but when more English lads kept turning up I began to get worried that they would keep me overnight and I would miss my coach back home. We were all given forms to sign which we thought were release forms, then once we had all done one we were told they were charge sheets. The next thing I knew I was getting charged with assault and was told that I was going to court. I couldn't believe what was happening, and kept thinking that as soon as someone comes from the British Embassy all this will get sorted out, but no one came. There were fifteen of us and we didn't receive a visit from the British consul for three days. When the bloke did finally turn up he just gave us a few leaflets and asked a few questions – name, address and stuff like that. I asked him if he could ring home for me and gave him a number to call, but I later found out he never even did that. At that stage I expected to see him again later that day, but that was it, the only visit.

The prison wasn't too bad, not what they made out in the press here. They kept us well away from the locals and we had our own exercise yard and a television in each cell. Watching the news I saw myself getting beaten by the police and thought that would help once I went to court, but there was no one provided for us to sort things like that out, so I had to write home in order to get the evidence sent over. A mate of mine had taped a news item that had the same footage and he sent it out, but the French said it never arrived. Bullshit. We managed to get English papers nearly every day, and that was when I first saw my face on the front page. It had turned into a total nightmare. If I had been 20 yards down the road all this would never have happened.

When I did go to court I was given the same female lawyer as this other lad, but she said it would look better if she only represented one of us while a mate of hers did the other one. The lad I was with bunged her £200, and as I had no money I was left with her mate who was a joke. I met him once before we went to court and he couldn't speak a word of English. My meeting with him consisted of him miming me throwing a bottle and me saying, no, I didn't throw a bottle. That was it, then he left. Great justice system that is!

On the day it went to court he never even spoke to me and just sat over the other side of the room. When the charge was read out a couple of new offences had been added. Originally I was being charged with assault and throwing a bottle, but now I had threatened a policeman and carried an iron bar as well. That had my chin hitting the ground. One of the lads had heard they could lock us up for three years for violence, and there I was totally unable to defend myself and now looking at all this. The judge and my so-called lawyer spoke to each other in French, and all I was asked was how I pleaded. I said not guilty, they said guilty, and that was it, 40 days total. There was nothing I could say and no one to turn to, which is bloody disgraceful. You hear stories like this all the time, but you wouldn't believe it possible unless you actually experienced it. Our own government didn't want to know.

There was another lad from Portsmouth who was in an even worse position than me because he had originally been with his wife and kids when he got pulled up. She didn't have a clue what had happened to him and didn't get to see him until three days later. She was well stuck and in a terrible state. They had a hire car but she couldn't drive. The kids didn't know what had hit them and her husband was in the cells. When we were in court she came to watch, and as she left she was spat at and kicked by the Tunisians that had come to see their mates get done. Thankfully she was saved from anything worse by an English press photographer who covered her head and got her to a taxi.

After a few days we got given some post, and the first letter I opened was from my work telling me I'd been suspended without pay. Three months later and I am still waiting for them to reinstate me, but I could still end up getting sacked as well. They sent the letter to the jail the minute they saw the picture of me on the front page and read what the government was saying about sacking anyone arrested in France. They didn't wait to hear my side of the story; just a short letter, no questions. It didn't matter that I hadn't done anything. I also got a letter from the Football Association telling me to send my membership card back. Again, they didn't want to hear my story. Ten years a member, then booted out. Cheers.

In the prison the locals were filthy, and although we were kept away from them they would throw sheets covered in shit over the fence into our yard, and used needles as well. They had a big drugs problem in there apparently. When Holland played Argentina down here a couple of Dutch guys were locked up as well, but those poor sods were put in with the locals, which must have been a nightmare. There was also some Algerian terrorist in one block and they thought we were great, because they hated the French I suppose.

Two days before we were due for release I had only my second contact with the British consul. They wrote me a letter telling me that if I was being deported then the French would put me on the first plane they could get. If not, I would need £200 to get home myself. It went on to say that if I didn't have the money then I should arrange to have it sent out. As I said, this letter only arrived two days before my release. Now, bearing in mind it took two days for post to get out of the prison, and another two days to clear anything sent to me, it was useless. I got kicked out of that place with £20 in my pocket and was issued a temporary passport with someone else's photo on it!

As soon as we got outside a reporter came up from a French paper and asked if we'd do an interview. Can you believe that? She soon got told where to go. Luckily, I was released with two others and one of them had a credit card. He paid for the train home, but when we got to Waterloo we got pulled in by the police because of the passport and questioned yet again. Some trip!

Now I am doing all I can to clear my name, but getting anything like paperwork out of the French is virtually impossible. I've got to keep trying though, else I could still lose my job. I've been banned from the club I've supported all my life, and I want that lifted. I am banned from entering France for two years, but I wouldn't go back there if you paid me anyway. And I want my name cleared so that I can get my England Travel membership back and not have a criminal record.

Now there's a story. Mr Mellor and chums, do your stuff. Go on, I dare you.

Calm Down, Calm Down: For God's Sake, Calm Down

Day 8: Wednesday, 17 June

The next morning I rose early and made my way downstairs to the breakfast room. I was carrying with me the worst hangover I'd had in years, and my mouth tasted like a baboon's arse the night after the said monkey had eaten the hottest vindaloo. I was first 'greeted' by the wife of the hotel manager as she slammed down a pot of black coffee in front of me and then turned away in disgust. I was then joined by the manager himself.

'Your friends, they are stupid.'

The banging in my head stopped me from answering, but I couldn't help wondering what the hell had happened now. It turned out that they had knocked him up at 4.00 a.m. because they were locked out of the hotel. The previous night he had given us a piece of paper with the security code for the door entry system written on it, and they couldn't remember the number. Once again he wrote down the number and gave it to me, but on inspection I soon realised that it was different from the one he had given us the previous day. I flicked through my wallet and picked out the piece of paper. As he realised his mistake the wife reappeared and clocked the number herself. You could see the anger rise through her body. Totally ignoring the fact that I was sitting in between them, she let rip. Her shouting banged through my delicate little head before she stormed off in the direction of the kitchen, with him chasing behind. As the shouting continued I decided that it was probably best that I pick myself up and go and find a quieter place to have breakfast.

If you're going to have a hangover then you could do a lot worse than have it in Palavas, but as I walked around this beautiful little port I thought for the first time of chucking it all in and heading back to England. I still had my train ticket, and there was plenty of time for me to get home, have a few days to myself and then get back out in time for the Romania game. After a solid hour of drinking coffee and fresh orange the decision was made, so I headed back to the hotel in order to get my things together.

As I entered the building the first people I saw were Barry and the lovely Tony. Once again, Tony spoke to me while looking in completely the opposite direction. Referring to the manager, he said, in all seriousness, 'Don't worry about him. He's all right today.' For some reason I couldn't help but laugh. What a total tosser. Tony began to laugh as well, and pretty soon the three of us were in fits. The wife of the owner soon appeared and began to apologise for her outburst earlier, and suddenly all thoughts of returning home were gone as talk turned to planning a day out in Montpellier.

By one o'clock Wiltshire, Tony, Barry and myself were heading off, leaving Mr B and Gary to catch up on some shut eye. Wiltshire had already got himself a ticket for the game as this was one match he really didn't want to miss. Many of the lads that followed his club back home were of Italian origin, and he really wanted to wind them up when he got back about seeing the *azzurri* in World Cup action when they hadn't.

Once again we found ourselves in a beautiful city with the sun beating down on our heads, and for the first time we got a real taste of what France '98 was like for all the other fans. The main square was a sea of colour as the Italians waved flags and the Africans danced and beat their drums. National dress was the order of the day for the Cameroonians and they brought a smile to the faces of everyone they came into contact with.

We walked past the big screen and into a tree-lined avenue that housed an exhibition and market demonstrating the local trades and delicacies. We were treated to tent after tent offering wine and food tasting, which, for four England lads on the ponce, was a total godsend. We were all thankful for the fact that obviously no Scousers had arrived here yet, as by now there would surely have been nothing left.

It is at times like these that you realise what the England fans are missing out on, and you have to wonder if we will ever get to experience hospitality such as this. I honestly doubt that we ever will. We all joked about what would happen if 10,000 England lads suddenly found themselves in a free drinking village, but the laughter was tinged with the fact that deep down we all really knew what would happen once the freebies eventually did run out.

You can only take the piss for so long before things start to get a little embarrassing, so we finally left the free food and wine behind and headed off up one of the back streets. In the distance we soon spotted a bar full of very noisy Italians and decided to get into the spirit of things and joined them for a beer. As it turned out, every one of them was from Australia, which went some way to explaining the noise level and the amount of beer that was being consumed. Our introduction was muted when, on hearing we were England fans, one lad began to give us grief for all the trouble that had gone on in Marseille. Now I am the first to admit that I have a slightly short fuse, but it rapidly becomes even shorter when people start talking complete bollocks about events they know nothing about, so pretty quickly I bit. Tony soon reminded me that it was their day and their match, so maybe this time it was best to bite my lip and sit at another table.

On finishing our drinks we headed back to the main square in time to catch Chile against Austria, and once we had positioned ourselves Wiltshire and I were allocated the job of hunting down a supermarket and getting the beers in.

It was while making our way through the crowd that I came across one of the most sickening things I witnessed during the whole of France '98. Crossing our path we spotted a group of lads wearing football shirts of the teams they supported back home, and as you do, we stopped and had a few quick words. Suddenly my brain caught up with my eyes and registered the fact that one of the lads in their group was wearing an Argentinian shirt. It wasn't until he joined the conversation that I actually realised he was with these lads, as at first I had thought he was just standing there waiting to get past.

This new craze for wearing other countries' colours is something I just cannot understand. It's bad enough seeing kids wearing Barcelona or Juventus shirts, but it really pains me to walk up my local high street and see kids in the Brazil and Dutch national kit. What parent in their right mind would allow his child to go out and spend his hard-earned wages on a German shirt? It is something that is totally beyond me.

As this lad butted in on the conversation I cut him short and asked him why he was wearing the sky blue and white stripes of Argentina. He replied by lifting his top and showing me the Liverpool shirt he had on underneath, saying, 'Well, I've got this on as well, haven't I?' When I asked him what he meant by that, he replied, 'Well, it's simple, isn't it?'

'Yeah, you're right. It's simple. You must be some kind of cunt.'

A few seconds' silence followed before his mates turned to walk off. Although Wiltshire totally agreed with my sentiments, he reminded me that this was the second time in little over an hour that I had bitten and had words with someone. The sudden realisation struck me that to any outsider watching I would have looked and acted in a manner that fitted every stereotypical view of an Englishman abroad, and there was nothing I could say to counter his observation.

The crowd in the main square cheered when they saw the Chilean national side belt out their national anthem once again. I really like this side, and when Salas scored with 20 minutes to go it appeared that the majority of those around me shared my feelings. The match was poor, more noticeable for the amazing seventies-style haircuts of the Austrians and the girlie headbands worn by some of the Chilean players than the football. Then, once again, a fantastic last-minute strike secured Austria another late point, and the South American flags at the front of the screen finally stopped waving. The final whistle went to signal the mass exodus towards the train station where the buses were waiting to take people up to the Stade de la Mosson, the venue for tonight's fixture.

Up at the ground we soon found that tickets were yet again both in demand and in the hands of the local Arabs. On this occasion the touts were using local kids as runners. The youngsters approached people wanting tickets and then disappeared for a few minutes before returning with the prize in hand. With 30 minutes to go before kick-off the price finally began to drop, but the atmosphere became more edgy. The locals were now starting to dip their hands in people's pockets, trying to steal anything they could get. An Italian fan standing next to us unfortunately dropped his ticket before suddenly finding himself swamped by kids grabbing away at the dirt. The few stiff cuffs around the ear he dished out were met with looks of real anger by the kids, and despite the age and obvious size difference you could see he felt well and truly worried for his safety.

The tickets had now fallen to around the £40 mark, and Barry managed to secure one at that price just before the sudden arrival of a busload of Japanese. Suddenly the price rocketed back up to over £100 as, following on from the ticket shambles the Japs had already experienced, they were prepared to pay whatever it took to get into a game. With the price rising by the second Tony and I jumped back on to a bus and headed back to town along with hundreds of others.

The atmosphere back at the big screen was excellent as supporters from all nations mixed with the locals and cheered on the two teams whenever the players did something extraordinary. Throughout the game Tony and I found ourselves standing next to two Plymouth fans who were busy working on getting the Australian girl they were with totally shit-faced. To tell the truth, it didn't look like they were having that much of a problem, and one of them soon explained that they had nowhere to stay and were hoping she would put them up for the night. They were also trying to convince her to let them pay her in kind, and from where I was standing it looked like they could well all be in for a long night and an embarrassing morning.

Seconds before the final whistle blew, three of the biggest skinheads I've ever seen brushed past me in order to get down to the front of the screen. All were wearing Lazio shirts and had swastika tattoos. They were probably three of the most evil-looking bastards you could ever meet, and in their wake they left a trail of people with a look of disbelief on their faces. The match ended in a rather flattering 3–0 win for Italy.

We had agreed to hook up with Wiltshire and Barry after the game at a bar known as the London Tavern, so we quickly headed off in that direction to find the place swamped with the same Sunderland and Newcastle fans we had travelled across from Marseille with. They had obviously been on a big all-day session and by the time we arrived were well and truly slaughtered. As they sat drinking outside the bar they sang at any group of fans that dared to join in their banter. As the crowds making their way up from the main square grew, the singing began to take on a slightly more offensive edge, and once the cry of 'Shit-alia!' went up I couldn't help but wonder what would happen if those Lazio skinheads suddenly made an appearance. To be fair, some of the lads in the group looked just as unhappy about the verbal as I was and began either to make their excuses and leave or head inside. It didn't take long for me to join them. It was interesting to note that while all the other bars we had visited that day were rammed with a mixture of fans, the only people drinking in this bar were English. But when you took into account the welcoming committee outside, you soon realised why.

We decided to wait inside until Barry and Wiltshire returned and once they had they soon told us that the game had been a bit of an anti-climax. Slowly but surely the bar began to fill up, and Wiltshire soon began to recognise some faces from his home town and from various trips with England. One of his friends was a dead ringer for Norman Bates out of the *Psycho* movie, and appeared to be just as mental. This lad was doing the rounds trying to get a mob of lads together to go outside with him and kick it off. Luckily no one wanted to take him up on the offer. He definitely had the look of a man who was not the full hamper, and at any moment I expected him to turn and smash the glass he was holding into my face just so that he could get the fix of violence he undoubtedly wanted. When I told this to Wiltshire he laughed and explained that he was the softest bloke you could meet, but somehow I didn't believe him. Another lad then made himself known to Wiltshire, and the two on meeting greeted each other like long-lost friends.

I was beginning to pick up on the fact that many of the lads that follow England to the far corners of the globe do so under their own steam. Wiltshire had already told us that he undertook many difficult trips by himself, as did Barry. Wiltshire's friend then went on to tell us that since they had last met he had witnessed the most hilarious pitch invasion he had ever seen. While working in Burkina Faso he had attended a match that, following a poor decision by the referee, quickly turned into a full-scale riot. The funny thing was that the trouble was sparked off by an invasion of disabled people from the wheelchair enclosure. We all know it's a terrible thing to take the piss out of disabled people, but when he told us that the rival fans then ran on from the other end and just tipped over the wheelchairs, we couldn't help but crack up laughing. Those wheelchair-bound hooligans were left squirming around on the floor unable to get themselves back up while the police came and arrested the lot of them.

To my surprise, we were then joined by a lad from, of all places, Wales. He was on his way back home after watching the Welsh national side play two friendly matches, one against Tunisia (which they lost) and one against Malta (which they won). He had decided to extend his trip by a few days so that he could take in a slice of France '98, and although he hated the English they were the only bastards that could understand him. There was no way he was going to tag along with a load of haggis shaggers, so he was making the best of a bad job. He supported Cardiff City, and when I announced that I enjoyed a deep-rooted hatred for Swansea City due to the fact that some of their fans very nearly kicked me to death once, he seemed to warm to me a little – although he had to laugh because, after all, I was English and probably deserved it. Like all Cardiff fans he soon began to moan about the club he loves, mentioning the fact that if someone were to put money into building up the club then their support base would be massive. As my mouth spouted out agreeing words of comfort, my mind was thinking more along the lines of, 'Yeah, but who cares?' But I thought it best that I just humour him and save myself a hiding.

Pretty soon the owner of the bar called time, so we got ourselves a taxi and headed home. On arriving back at Palavas we soon found Mr B and Gary propping up a bar and looking rather the worse for wear. After joining them for six or seven more nightcaps I made my way back to the hotel, only to find that my fingers and brain had fallen out. This unfortunate lack of personal body control made it impossible for me to punch in the entry phone numbers, so once again the owner found himself knocked out of bed at gone four in the morning. Still, fuck it, we were leaving in the morning anyway.

Touts and Tensions Rising
Day 9: Thursday, 18 June

Today I was woken early by the sound of Gary banging around in the room. When I finally managed to focus behind my eyes I noticed that he was fully dressed and had his rucksack in his hand. I asked him what he was doing, and to my surprise he replied that today he had decided to go back home. It turned out that Gary had told his wife he was only coming out for the one game, and she had expected him home on Tuesday morning. Yesterday, under a cloud of guilt, he had rung her for the first time and received the mother of all ear bashings. She also told him that she had found his ticket for the Colombia game, and that if he didn't get home pretty sharpish she would introduce the ticket to the scissors. Mr B was just sat up in bed laughing.

Gary and his missus were childhood sweethearts and had been married for over ten years. This wasn't the first time that Gary had pulled strokes like this on his wife, but she always stuck by him as he was a master at spinning tales that made her feel a little less cheated. This time the story went that Mr B had got him to France under false pretences and had bought him a rail pass and booked the hotels without Gary knowing. Gary told his wife that he didn't know what to do as Mr B had shelled out so much money, and so reluctantly he had stayed. Mr B, although a long-time friend of Gary, never had any dealings with his wife and so was more than happy to take the flak on his behalf. A quick goodbye and a promise to meet up in Lens, ticket permitting, and Gary was gone.

Within an hour we were also being waved off, only this time by the rather relieved hotel owner, who quickly locked the door behind us as we went. The plan today was to head for Toulouse, as this was the venue for England's next match. We felt that if we arrived in the city a few days before the main bulk of the England fans we might find getting a ticket that much easier.

Once again, we found the TGV rammed with football fans as we headed west. We were soon joined in the buffet by a young lad who looked worse than Rod Hull after a fall-out with Emu, rough as fuck and down on his luck. When we realised he was English we began talking to him, and soon found out why he appeared to be in such a state.

J. was from Manchester, and back in England earned his living as a ticket tout. He had come to France hoping to make a killing and very quickly found himself well ahead on the money, but while he was working outside the Parc des Princes for the Germany v. USA game things took a turn for the worse. He was doing a deal with an American guy who was really taking his time about getting the money together to pay for a ticket. As J. tried to hurry him up and reached for the money, he suddenly found a set of handcuffs whacked around his wrists, and before he knew it he was being frog-marched away by a special team of police officers. At the time J. had over £3,000 and 30 tickets for various games on him, and after being taken to a quiet area and searched was offered a deal. He had to either hand over the cash and the tickets no questions asked, or he could spend the next three months in a French nick and then have the money and tickets taken away legally. Pretty soon he found himself back out on the street but somewhat lighter. He was left with a little over £100 in his pocket and about ten tickets that had been tucked in his pants when he got lifted.

I hate to say it, but my first impression of J. was not to trust him, but after hearing his story and talking to him about his trade I soon warmed to him as he turned out to be a top bloke. He explained that getting tugged by the police was always a risk, but over the years he had managed to avoid them more than most of his colleagues. I was also surprised to hear him say that back home the tout is not looked upon nowadays with such contempt. He believed this was due to the fact that for many people the tout was their only hope of getting to see the team they supported. Getting the odd slap was also part of the gig, but that too was tending to become less of a risk. He explained that although he worked alone, many of the touts worked in very organised gangs, and dishing out a kicking to a tout would soon have ten or more of his mates arriving to return the favour. Touting tickets was all he had ever done. He couldn't bear the thought of a steady job, and I have no doubt that he loved the excitement that went with his work. He also told us that up in Paris the German fans had really given the French riot police a hard time and that there had been more than a few rucks.

While in the buffet we also met an Asian lad from London who was using the French rail network in order to get to as many games as possible. He told us that he had applied to the Football Association for as many tickets as they would let him have. He knew he was only likely to get one England ticket, so he put a cross in every box available for all the other games and had come up trumps with tickets for nine different matches. Today he was taking in South Africa v. Denmark before travelling overnight to Saint Etienne so that he could watch Spain play Paraguay tomorrow. He had booked every rail journey in advance so that wherever possible he would be sleeping while travelling through the night, thus saving on hotel bills. When J. heard how he had managed to get so many tickets he looked more than a little pissed off that he hadn't thought of the same scam. And when the Asian lad realised J. was a tout, he very quickly tucked his wallet full of tickets back inside his jacket pocket.

Word had been out that the mayor of Toulouse had wanted

to ban the England fans from coming to town, but now it was being said that we would be made welcome in a city that is known more for its love of rugby than football. All rumours were soon kicked into touch as we soon found out from the tourist information office that the city with the most hotels was completely booked up – well, if you had an English accent it was, anyway. The best we were offered was a room in a small town over 15 miles out from the city centre, so we left the station and sat ourselves down in the first bar we came to in order to discuss what we should do next.

While in the station J. had managed to buy four tickets for today's game between South Africa and Denmark at the face value of £40 each, but following an approach to us by an American guy he soon realised that he should have waited an hour or so to suss out the ticket situation. The American guy who had approached us immediately asked if we wanted tickets for the game. He had as many tickets as we needed and all were at face value. At this stage I wanted to make sure that I got to see at least one World Cup game, and as I wasn't holding out that much hope of getting to see England I took him up on the offer along with Tony and Mr B. The name stamped on the tickets was once again that of the American company I had encountered before. The tout also told us to keep our eyes open for him on the day of the England game as he would hopefully be back in Toulouse with more match tickets. He went on to say that he was working for an agent who would ring him up early in the evening and tell him what city to head for. He didn't know from one day to the next what tickets he would be told to pick up and then sell, but he was working every day and doing very nicely by the look of him.

For us, the next major hurdle to overcome was that of finding somewhere to stay, but to my surprise and annoyance no one else seemed that bothered, so I headed off on my own in the hope of finding a bed for the night. After an hour or so of being turned away I managed to find us a hotel that was fully booked for tonight but had two rooms for the following three, so I decided to take a chance and booked them both. I returned to find the lads at the same bar, and although they were more than happy with my efforts, unlike me they were also happy to sleep rough on the streets tonight, now safe in the knowledge that they could shower and crash out all day tomorrow.

Time was now getting tight if we were to get up to the stadium to make kick-off, so we headed for the Metro. Following a further short bus ride we found ourselves up at the Stade Municipal, a beautiful ground set in the middle of an island. Walking up towards the stadium the road was lined with people desperately trying to sell tickets, and although I had only paid face value for mine I couldn't help but feel a little ripped off.

Inside the ground the atmosphere was good, but I have to say that unless I am watching Watford or England I often find football a little boring. Denmark were absolutely shite, and just how they managed to get a point out of this game I'll never know. The lasting memory I will have from this game is the fact that it had to be played under the hottest sun I've ever experienced. You know things are getting a little dodgy when the heat even has South Africans fainting all around you, and as the sun was burning down directly onto the section I was sitting in, I began to question my decision of wearing dark blue jeans and T-shirt.

The previous day Sepp Blatter, the FIFA president, had issued a warning to the referees to get tougher on the tackle from behind, so in a desperate bid to secure the job of the final the man in charge for this game, Señor Rendón, sent three off for fuck all, but at least it provided some entertainment. Following the final whistle Marc Rieper of Denmark was quoted as saying, 'Any more matches like ours will kill the World Cup.' I don't know whether he was talking about the refereeing or the actual game, but I didn't exactly feel ecstatic when I left the ground either.

In the toilet at half-time I began talking to Steve, an Arsenal fan. I would like to point out here that I don't usually like talking to people in public toilets as I am not oversure of their motives, and so at first I was a little suspicious about him. But once we had both shaken and zipped up, I felt a little more at ease, and he went on to tell me a great little hobby he and his mates had started up during the last domestic season.

As his beloved Gunners marched to the title, an added slice of happiness for them was the fact that their great rivals Spurs were doing so badly. Whenever they lost, he and his friends had taken to telephoning the David Mellor radio phone-in programme pretending to be disgruntled Tottenham fans. They would pick on particular players and slaughter them live on air in the hope that it would dent their confidence even more, before going on to tell the country that things were being made worse for them by the fact that the Gunners were doing so well – in fact, the Gunners were brilliant! One of his friends had even phoned the programme and admitted that he had gone to watch Arsenal on the sly with a mate and that the football was so good that he was now considering not going back to White Hart Lane, as the visit to Highbury had made him realise just how bad Spurs had become. How simple – pure genius.

Quite why I have never thought of doing this myself I do not know, but I shall certainly be trying it out for my own pleasure in the very near future. I don't like Mr Mellor, and I don't like his programme. How many times have I heard the words, 'No, I wasn't actually at the game, but ... '? In my opinion the show is both hosted by, and provides, the ultimate tool. A tool with which to ridicule not only the man himself but the teams we call the scum at the same time. After discovering this lad's hobby I believe it's mine and every other fan's duty to try to emulate Steve's success. On those beautiful days when the Hornets win and the scum lose my fingers will definitely be doing the walking as well as the reversed 'V' sign.

Once the game was over we headed back to the centre of the city. As we made our way back to the bus stop I came across a Norwegian guy offering a ticket for the England game against Romania, but the £300 he wanted was certainly more than I, or any of the others, was prepared to pay. On returning to the city centre J. suddenly spotted a friend of his from Manchester who was also a tout by trade, and like J. he was also finding France '98 hard going. Not only had the local French people got more than their fair share of the tickets, but they were not willing to sell them on for anything less than the top price. He told J. that he and another lad were driving up to Nantes as that was the venue for Japan's next match. He had a few dodgy tickets and the news had travelled fast that the Japs were willing to pay almost any price asked without really knowing what they were buying. J. was more than welcome to join him on the journey, so he grabbed his bag and left us and Toulouse behind.

My mind quickly turned back to the problem of finding somewhere to stay. Once again I headed off to find a room for the evening on my own. By now I couldn't really give a toss about where the others ended up as they continued to show no interest, so it was looking after number one time. After another half hour's searching I came across a hotel run by a guy who refused even to try to communicate in anything other than French, not even a hello. I worked out that he had one room for two people, so I booked myself in and decided that the others could fight it out among themselves for the other bed. After a few minutes of flicking coins, Mr B ended up as my room-mate for the night, and to my annoyance Wiltshire and Tony decided that they would just bunk in anyway, which once again had the tension rising inside me. As we reluctantly tried to sneak their bags into the room, the watchful owner sussed out the scam and threatened to throw us all out onto the street, but this time the language barrier came in handy as I pleaded ignorance, and we managed to calm the situation down.

The events of the past few days, along with the constant stream of lager, had finally begun to catch up with me; all I wanted to do was shower and fall into bed, but the others had different ideas. Wiltshire had decided that the best way to get through a night sleeping rough on the streets was to get absolutely shit-faced so that eventually he would just pass out and fall down in a heap somewhere, not caring. This suggestion appeared to sit quite nicely with Tony's plans, so off we went for a quick nightcap. In a bar we heard that France had qualified for the second phase following a 4–0 win over Saudi Arabia, a result that brought about the first managerial sacking of the tournament, that of Saudi coach Carlos Alberto Parreira. That'll teach the man who led Brazil to victory in '94 to get above his station. This win for France was a shit because the sooner they got knocked out the sooner the locals would lose interest in the tournament, thus leaving more tickets up for grabs.

Following a swift drink, Mr B and I head home leaving the others to find themselves a late bar and a shop doorway for the night. I couldn't help but feel guilty and pissed off with them at the same time. I was pissed off because they never even made the effort and didn't think twice about the possibility of getting me thrown out as well, but guilty because while I was safely tucked up they were out wandering the streets. Still, fuck 'em.

Back home, the English football supporters had found them-selves a rather unexpected friend in Tory MP Alan Clark, whose comments on the violence of Marseille are seen as being more than a little misplaced. He is reported as saying, 'In a sense, that is a kind of compliment to the English martial spirit . . . Football matches are now a substitute for the old medieval tournaments. They are by nature aggressive and confront-ational.' And when asked if he thinks it is OK to pick up a bottle thrown at you and then throw it back, he says, 'It certainly is.'

Well I never! The picture printed in the *Mirror* of the MP's head pasted onto the body of an English hooligan is a classic, as are the words of support Mr Clark receives from the Marchioness of Reading: 'The so-called hooligans are just over-enthusiastic . . . We are a nation of yobs. And now we don't have a war, what's wrong with a good punch up? . . . I rejoice in the fact that there are people who keep up our historic spirit.' The words 'mad' and 'cow' spring to mind, but one further remark leaves a glimmer of hope for us all: 'Maybe I am wicked and dangerous and ought to be put down.' Please form an orderly queue.

Fuck Football, Let's Dance
Day 10: Friday, 19 June

All my feelings of guilt towards Tony and Wiltshire disappeared in a split second at precisely six a.m. when I was woken by the telephone next to my bed. The voice on the other end of the line was Wiltshire asking us to come down and let them in. They had been trying to convince the woman who had taken over on reception that they had been locked out, and although she had seen through their story she agreed to let them into the hotel as long as we were all out by midday, as that was when the owner was due back. Within five minutes the two lads were up in the room and snoring like elephants. The noise from Tony's hooter drove me so mad that eventually I had to get out of my pit and give the bed over to him.

I got dressed and unbelievably found myself walking the streets at seven o'clock in the morning instead of those two tits. At this time I hit my lowest point of the trip so far, and once again I made up my mind to get the first train back home and leave them all behind. If this went on much longer Tony and I were going to have one major fall-out, and deep down I really didn't want that. Although at this stage I thought the man to be the most inconsiderate prick I had ever had the misfortune to meet, I still kind of liked him in a strange way. That, coupled with the fact that he stood over a foot taller than myself, had me thinking that a fight was probably not that good an idea.

After wandering the empty streets for an hour or so I returned to the hotel for breakfast in time to see a most wondrous sight. As I sat down with only my bread, jam and coffee for company, two South African gentlemen entered the room and placed themselves at the next table. We quickly began talking about their game against Denmark the previous day. They soon told me that they had been flown out to France by their employers, a wine company, and they were enjoying the free trip of a lifetime.

As the conversation continued we were joined by a third gentleman whose arrival stopped the conversation dead, for he was wearing the worst and most ill-fitting wig I have ever seen. I swear the chunk of bread I was chewing fell from my open mouth on seeing this quite unbelievable hairpiece. His fellow countrymen just stared at me to gauge my reaction, and quite how they stopped themselves from choking I will never know. Now, I don't know whether the rug wearer was in some kind of hurry to get to breakfast or what, but this thing on his head looked more like an extra-large cycle helmet that was on back to front. It was so large and badly placed that when he turned to talk to me the thing remained pointing in the original direction. After a minute or so I managed to divert my stare and looked towards his colleagues for reassurance, only to find both of them staring down at their breakfast plates unable to make contact for fear of letting go. I wanted to call the world and have them come and see. Just who this man was trying to kid I will never know, and after a few minutes I could take no more and left the room. As I walked up the corridor it took all my strength not to shout back at him 'WIGGY!' but I managed to hold it together just in time to make the lift before bursting out laughing. That encounter, and the looks on those guys' faces, provided me with a memory that will live as long as any of the other events that had already passed by me on this trip.

Later that morning the four of us left the hotel and headed

for our next abode. At first I couldn't even bring myself to speak to the others and continually mulled over in my head different ways of heading off. The main thing that kept me in Toulouse that day was the fact that I had arranged to hook up with my brother Greg, who was still in France touring with the singer Natalie Imbruglia and her band. As it turned out they had a gig in Toulouse that night and were arriving today from just over the border in Spain. Thankfully, this provided me with the perfect excuse to get away and have some time on my own, so once we had checked in and unpacked I headed off to find the hotel in which Greg was staying.

To my surprise, Tony and Wiltshire knew the exact location of the hotel as they had managed to sneak into that very building the night before. The Sofotel is probably the most exclusive hotel in the city, and I couldn't help but be impressed by the fact that these two pissheads had managed to fool the security into thinking they were serious paying punters. The two of them went on to explain that they had checked out all the floors before finding a room with the door open and going inside. Tony had immediately dived on the bed and crashed out while Wiltshire took the floor. After about an hour Tony was rudely woken by the true occupant of the room, who seemed a little pissed off at the fact that someone else was in his bed. The sight of Wiltshire's head popping up from behind the wardrobe had made the room owner shit himself, which gave them enough time to escape before security finally caught up with them and escorted them gently but firmly from the building.

As I arrived at the hotel I could see three or four camera crews positioned outside, waiting. The target for their questioning was to be the English Football Association's head of security, Brian Hayes. On questioning the pressmen I found out that they seemed to think our Brian had thrown in the towel and admitted that he and his cronies were powerless to control the England fans and was now trying to divert the blame onto the French. At first I thought of hanging around as this could turn out to be fun, but following a few pointed questions to me along the lines of, 'What have you been involved in so far, then?' I suddenly remembered what a bunch of tossers English journalists were, so I spun them a quick yarn about a row up a back street with a gang of 20 locals before heading inside to find my brother.

I was soon told that the band was not due to arrive for another five hours, so I left my hotel contact number and buggered off for a walk around the centre of the city. As I left the foyer the elusive Brian was just arriving. As the lights flashed I could see a couple of the journalists were torn between getting him and trying to catch up with me for some more dirt on the row that never happened. Jokingly, I just gave them the two-fingered salute before jogging off down the road laughing.

I was to learn later that this very hotel was the centre of a ticket tout operation, which is a shame because if I had known I could have asked our Brian to put the word out for me. It was also reported that a ticket company based in Paris had been broken into the previous night and had 15,000 match tickets stolen. The poor company involved was the same one whose name was printed on the ticket I had purchased for the Denmark game yesterday!

Toulouse really is a beautiful city, and once again, as long as I tried to communicate with them in their own language, I found the French people more than polite towards me and very helpful. On entering one clothes shop I began talking to the assistant who, as it turned out, had studied in England and really enjoyed his time there – well, almost all of it, anyway. He told me that he loved London and Chester but had ended up working one summer in a town that was full of backward people and weirdos. He said the people all appeared to be living in the past, and the joke among all the other students he worked with was that the locals all slept with their close relations and that explained why they were so slow. The place in question? Swindon, Wiltshire's home town. Lovely! To my surprise I noticed that the clothes in his shop were much cheaper than the usual asking price in London, but he went on to tell me that these type of clothes were only worn by French kids who were seen as time wasters and drop-outs, and those who had little money. As I was actually wearing those very same surfing labels at that moment I suddenly felt a little deflated myself, so I left the shop.

I returned to the hotel some four hours later to find the now suspected closet inbred Wiltshire spark out on the bed, next to him a message from my brother telling me the venue and the time of tonight's gig. I quickly decided that for once I would have a night away from the football and booked a taxi before asking the others whether or not they wanted to tag along.

During the afternoon I watched yet another boring game, this time between Nigeria and Bulgaria, which the Africans won 1–0. So far the actual football has been a let-down; no real exciting teams and little in the way of atmosphere. During this match the Bulgarian players Stoitchkov and Kostadinov were booed throughout by the French crowd, who remembered their country's last-minute defeat by the Bulgarians in Paris that cost them qualification for USA '94. This proving that the French, like elephants, have not only big noses but long memories as well. By eight I was all togged up and heading off out for a rather different evening.

Although meeting up with my brother was good, the concern he displayed about my safety only rammed home the messages that were being sent out to the rest of the world about the England fans. One of the French crew on the tour soon started talking bollocks, asking me what the problem was with us English. He wanted to know why we couldn't behave like the rest of the world and have a good time, rather than wanting to smash everything up. His constant whinging really began to annoy me, but for the sake of my brother's career I thought it best I kept shtum.

By the time we returned to the city centre all the bars were being shut down by the police, so we headed back to the hotel in order to hit the minibar. As we walked along, a group of four French lads were walking in the opposite direction on the other side of the road. On seeing us one of the lads started shouting and slagging off the English. As he began to cross the road towards me I went to meet him halfway and held out my hand as a gesture of friendship, but he went to slap it away.

'Are you an English hooligan? I hate English. If you make trouble here we kill you.'

Bit strong, I thought. The aggression in his voice was there for all to hear. His friends, however, were far less happy at his outburst and sensed the worst. They quickly dragged him back and began to apologise for his actions. I replied to them by saying that we were not hooligans and we just wanted to have a good time like them, but once again the mouthy lad piped up with the threats, and this time went for me. Luckily his friends managed to hold him back before apologising once more and dragging him away. Wiltshire couldn't believe that I hadn't bitten the bullet and that I had just let it go without any real confrontation. The truth of the matter is that I had seen enough already on this trip, and I certainly didn't need any grief myself. A good few years back when I was a young lad the story might well have had a different ending. Those French lads should be thankful that their pal didn't pick on the wrong lads that night.

Incidents like that tread a very fine line. If a row had started, and let's say that one or two of them, or us for that matter, had ended up in hospital, then the whole feeling in that city could have changed completely. The press would have had all the headlines they needed and the riot police would have been put immediately on edge. Thankfully we had the sense to turn the other cheek and just walk away, but it could have been different, as no one likes being offered out or having their hand slapped away.

Back at the hotel, Mr B told us that he felt those lads that had tried to kick it off were in fact undercover police out looking for England fans to pull over, as they didn't look or act like any other French lads we had met so far. It is true to say that the streets were full of police cars and vans that night as the authorities went about closing all the bars by midnight, and in fact the more we thought about it the more likely his suspicion seemed to be true. While talking things over we sat and watched the highlights as Spain struggled to draw 0–0 with Paraguay in a match that virtually killed off their chances of qualifying for the next round. One of the tournament favourites had bitten the dust before they had even played all three of their first-round matches. At last, the World Cup was beginning to throw up surprises. Our only hope was that England didn't go the same way.

Day 11: Saturday, 20 June

Before I start today's entry, here's a quick question for all you trivia buffs: Who was the only player in an FA Cup semi-final to score a first-half hat-trick, then go in goal midway through the second half and save a penalty to secure a 3–2 victory?

Today was Mr B's birthday, so an all-day piss-up was soon given the thumbs up by way of celebration. By eleven o'clock we were firmly situated in one of the bars opposite the train station and beginning to stretch our ever-growing beer bellies.

This was the day that the expected invasion of England fans finally began to happen in Toulouse as a steady stream of fans from Blighty, out for the big weekend, arrived on the overnight trains. The initial shock and surprise at not being able to find a room was there to see on the face of every Englishman that passed the bar, and if we were asked for directions or spare tickets once, we were asked a thousand times.

After a few early-morning jars we made our way down to an English-owned pub called the Melting Pot, situated on a main drag halfway between the station and the main city square. This pub was to become a honey pot for the English fans over the next few days as well as the subject of much media attention. The general feeling we got from the journalists in our hotel was that if it were going to kick off, then we would kick off here.

We arrived at the bar just in time for the match between Japan and Croatia to start, a match that provided added interest following the news that the Japanese players had received a shipment of pornographic magazines in their training camp to help relieve the tension of the 'no sex before football' policy introduced by their coach. Obviously expecting a rather 'limp-wristed' affair, I was surprised by what turned out to be a fantastic game. The Japs were a far better side than most people had expected and gave the Croats a fair few scares during the first 45 minutes.

The tables next to me were soon taken up by a group of lads from Bristol who, to my total surprise, were a mix of Rovers and City fans. On hearing this I just couldn't pass up the opportunity of getting these lads arguing among themselves, and I tell you, it didn't take much. I started by letting the City lads give it the big one about their team's promotion while digging away at their mates' team's failure to make the play-off final. Then I hit them with the fact that I was a Watford fan, reminding them that we won the Championship and that they were in fact a shitty second best. This, of course, much to the delight of the previously ridiculed Rovers lads. To even up the contest I then got them going head to head about their various stadiums, and the fact that Rovers played at such a shit hole. Then, as I happily listened to the verbal battle, one of the City fans dropped a major bollock as far as I was concerned. He mentioned the fact that Rovers were better off when they played at Bath City's ground, Twerton Park, than they are now. This comment made my ears prick up even more as I have a strong liking for Bath City Football Club. He then went on to mention a firm of City lads who once took it upon themselves to try to burn down the main stand at Twerton as a way of getting at Rovers and their fans. This group of lads became known as the Bristol City Fire Brigade, and by their actions they very nearly killed a cleaner who was still working in the building at the time. On hearing this I bit and gave the lad a right mouthful. The truth is that I have always preferred Rovers, mainly due to the fact that an old school teacher of mine was a City fan and insisted on having a team poster up on the classroom wall. I happened to think him a total cunt, so I hated everything that was associated with him, this minor irritant obviously playing a major part in my thinking towards the red half of Bristol.

As my verbal grew more intense, fuelled by the angst of my teenage years, Tony suddenly piped up telling me not to look around. In my anger I had failed to notice that the pub had fallen silent. It turned out that while our heated conversation had developed a film crew had entered the bar and at this moment the cameraman was busy filming the back of my bald head. Now I am not over keen on being filmed without being asked at the best of times, but the fact that I was just sitting inside a bar, having a quietish drink and minding my own business made me slightly unhappy and highly suspicious. I didn't like the fact that I didn't have a clue who he was or even what he was after. We had already been told the rumours that police snatch squads had been brought into town from both England and Marseille, and that they were picking people out at random to be checked up on and possibly shipped straight back home.

Over the years there have been many cases of innocent fans falling foul to this treatment, and for all I knew I was their next victim. I purposefully kept my face pointing away from the lens as Wiltshire, Mr B and Tony left the bar to wait for me outside. I asked the lads from Bristol to tell me when the cameraman had grown tired, and as soon as they gave me the nod I got up and left the bar before the cameraman had time to lift his lens and catch my face. The West Country lads were left open-mouthed by what they saw. As I made my way out of the bar I heard one of them say, 'Fucking hell, them four must be heavy!' His words, of course, could not have been more wide of the mark. The truth was that we hadn't been involved in any trouble, but when you're abroad with England that doesn't necessarily mean you won't get deported. For all we knew they may well have been a local film crew, but even so I didn't want my face being used as 'the typical English football fan' on French television that night. Years of experience soon tell you never to trust film crews, no matter what you are doing. And you can believe me when I tell you that we were not the only lads to make a hasty exit from the Melting Pot at that moment.

Down at the main square the English had started to make their presence felt, and flags were laid out for all to see. The disturbing sight of a small mob of local African lads in Tunisian shirts soon had me thinking of what might happen. The film crews that were following their every move had these locals playing up to the role even more, but thankfully no one really paid them that much attention. Everyone we spoke to was looking for tickets, and at this stage the asking price was no lower than £300 – far higher than anyone was willing to pay.

You could still feel the unease in the air as the bar owners and restaurateurs of Toulouse expected the worst, but as more and more English arrived the vibe actually became better rather than worse. As the afternoon passed we watched one of the best games of the tournament so far, Mexico coming from 2–0 down to snatch a draw with Belgium. Mexico's second goal was an outstanding strike by Blanco that had the people in the bar rising to their feet in appreciation. As the rest of us applauded this unbelievable show of skill, Tony, unimpressed by what he had just seen, muttered under his breath that technically speaking the lad should have finished off the move with his other boot. You had to laugh. I couldn't help thinking that if only Mexico started playing before they were two goals down they could well turn out to be the surprise package of this World Cup, as their brand of football was as exciting as anything else I had seen so far.

Like the Japanese, those boring bastards the Belgians also found themselves under the cloud of 'no sex before matches'. However, the story was that the defender Eric Deflandre had hatched the cunning plan of bringing his very own blow-up doll to the tournament to help pass those long summer nights.

I couldn't help thinking that surely the end result of such activity is the same, so why not just let the girlfriends in for a good tonking? But as coaches insist on such measures I can only thank my lucky stars that for Orville's sake Keith Harris never made it as a professional footballer.

Wandering through the square on our way to yet another watering hole, I bumped into the two lads from Plymouth I had met in the square at Montpellier. They quickly informed me that, yes, they did stay with the Aussie bird and that although one of them had crashed out in the cab on the way back the other did do the deed and paid for the rent in kind. By all accounts it was very nice as well, and it was all topped off with a good breakfast in the morning. Bastards.

As darkness fell the police presence suddenly grew, and once again many of the English fans went on the defensive as rumours of snatch squads began to circulate. We made our way back towards the Melting Pot bar and sat ourselves down in the Belgian pub opposite in the hope of seeing some familiar faces across the road. We watched as Holland hammered the South Koreans 5–0, and to my surprise I found myself sitting next to a Watford fan I had never seen before, but who knew all the same people as me. And being a Watford lad he had managed to fall in shit and come out smelling of roses.

He was actually sitting with a French girl he had pulled in a bar in Marseille. Since they had met she had put him up rent free, paid for his train to Toulouse and was footing the bill for their current hotel. The young lady on his arm spoke very little English, so we were able to hold a normal conversation without her having a clue as to what he was saying about her. She just smiled back as we agreed on the fact that, well, she wasn't exactly an oil painting, but his reply that you should never look a gift horse in the mouth was hard to argue against. 'Horse' being the appropriate word. The things people do in the name of England!

Fuelled by beer, the England fans began to sing their songs louder and louder as they spilled from the Melting Pot and onto the main road. The sight of well-to-do French families sitting in the street cafés opposite while eating beautifully presented seafood seemed a little bizarre following the arrival of the riot police. It appeared that the French had a fascination with the England fans that led them to bring out their entire families in order to stand on street corners and watch us get shit-faced. It is obvious the English and the Scots are different to our cousins across the water, but maybe instead of just watching us they should join in. Who knows, they may even like it.

By midnight we were moved on as the police began closing the bars once more, so we ducked down a side street and found one last drinking hole before heading home. The one thing I had learnt above all others this day was that Tony wasn't the complete arse I had him down for. Although he would admit he was hard work, he made me realise that I was just as bad, if not worse. Whereas he had been taking the piss out of me and himself, I had been taking it all a little too seriously. As ever when a group of pissed-up blokes get together, the subject of sex popped its head up and the lanky one had us in fits as he explained his sexual preferences. He also told us that he only dated supermodels and had never been out with an ugly woman in his life. He kind of shot himself in the foot as he went on to describe his dream date as Louise Woodward, although they wouldn't have kids of course. He was sure that if she just got to see him then that would be it; the girl would be rendered powerless by his good looks and undoubted charm.

He also informed me of my new nickname: Ceefax. As far as he was concerned, I was a mine of useless information. This led to Wiltshire and Tony entering into a quiz on their knowledge of the great game that lasted until we finally made our way back to the hotel. On every correct answer he made, Tony would add, 'I am telling you, I know my football.'

It was near the beginning of this quiz that Tony offered up the question I asked at the beginning of this chapter. After a solid hour's frustration, Tony finally gave us the answer: Roy of the Rovers, Melchester, 1968. Bastard.

And So To War
Day 12: Sunday, 21 June

During the build-up to France '98, this day above all others was billed by the world's press as the day of reckoning as Germany took on Yugoslavia and Iran played the USA.

As we sat in a quiet bar way down in the south of France, a firm of German hooligans was busy causing havoc on the streets of Lens. The Germans had already shown their colours at their first game in Paris, and, fuelled by a meeting in a country with which they have a highly provocative past, they went to town. While in Paris they had proved that as far as they were concerned the French riot police were there to be fought, not something to be scared of. Whipped up by the press back home, which had made use of constant references to the war such as the insulting phrase 'whip them away', a reference to the German invasion of Yugoslavia over 50 years ago, their mob was once again on the rampage.

The Yugoslavs also played their part during the build-up, referring to the fixture as 'more than a football match – this is war', so the scene was well and truly set. The horrific images showing a policeman being beaten around the head brought home to many the extent of what was once known as 'the English disease'. I am not making excuses for any of the English lads that had come to France looking for trouble, and as I've said before there were plenty that had, but this incident shocked me and many others more than the events they had personally witnessed in Marseille. The French were fully aware that this match above all others would provide the police with a stiff test, as is illustrated in this extract from a letter I received two months before the tournament even kicked off. Axel from Paris wrote:

Paris will see much trouble as there are many poor African people in the city as well as the Boulogne Boys from Paris Saint Germain. Holland and Belgium will be a big test for the Paris boys, and when Germany play here also. We know that hooligans from Kaiserslautern will come to all Germany matches, but all hooligans from Germany will go to Lens for the match with Yugoslavia. They are very organised. The police are very worried about this game more than all the others. More so than England and Tunisia. Also, the threat from terrorists from Iran when they play USA is a very big worry.

The violence that erupted in Lens provided the evidence that no matter how prepared or pre-warned the authorities are it is almost impossible to stop those that wish to indulge in violence from doing so. The account given in the media by a 17-year-old German arrested at the incident makes chilling reading:

I saw one of us break his weapon in two pieces and then smash the cop over the head with the butt. They all kicked at him and beat him. They went at him like animals. There were 50 of us, the hard core, marching through the city centre shouting: 'We are Germans. We're scared of nothing. Let's get the cops.' Anybody who wasn't German got thumped.

The violence was on such a scale that over 80 people were arrested, and the incident that left one policeman in a coma jolted the German Football Association into offering the World

Cup committee their resignation from the tournament. This gesture, although honourable, would only have been seen as a victory for these hooligans as their notoriety would have travelled the world and lived in the history books for ever. No matter what people try to introduce into the game it is inevitable that politics, violence and football will always have an unwelcome union. Thankfully, at the time of writing I know that the policeman who was hospitalised has now recovered from the coma he was so violently put into. Thank God. Unfortunately, I have to add that undoubtedly his experience, and that of his family, will not be the last of its kind.

We sat through the game between these two nations totally oblivious to what was happening on the streets. The actual match provided everything the football fan could hope for as the ever efficient Germany clawed their way back from 2–0 down to snatch a draw with an equaliser just ten minutes from time.

Following on from yesterday's all-day drinking session it was decided that today we should pace ourselves and get some serious food down our necks. Indecision followed, much to Tony's annoyance, until finally he'd had enough and dragged us into a steak restaurant. Although the food was no good for me, I sat and watched as they munched their way through the best part of a cow before we headed off to find somewhere to watch the Argies play Jamaica. We hadn't got twenty yards from the restaurant door before Tony gave out the loudest and most horrible retching noise I have ever heard. In broad daylight, on a main road and in the clear view of all those enjoying their al fresco afternoon meal, Tony threw out the steak he had just eaten like the girl possessed in *The Exorcist*. As he bellowed out at the top of his voice you could see people throwing down their knives and forks in total disgust while we fell about. Wiltshire was almost sick himself trying not to laugh. Was there nothing this man did quietly? Wiltshire offered the question as to how noisy Tony was while shagging, but as he looked up, with dribbles of puke hanging off his chin, all he could do was offer a few well-chosen words: 'Fuck off.'

Once Tony had cleaned himself up we found ourselves a bar where we met up with a group of lads from Bristol we kept bumping into throughout our stay. They were the first to tell us about the policeman in a coma, and they said that they were beginning to feel like they had had enough of the whole thing. They told me that if anything started here then they were off. They put the idea in my head that the Glastonbury music festival was starting next week, and that it would be better to watch the England v. Colombia game and have a drink there rather than deal with even more hassle, and I have to admit it did sound a good proposition. We witnessed the Argies stuff the Jamaicans 5–0, and to my secret delight Batistuta scored a hat-trick, making him the leading scorer and making my pre-tournament bet look like a safe one.

Everywhere you looked you were guaranteed to see an Englishman walking around aimlessly with a bag slung over his shoulder, desperate for somewhere to sleep. Toulouse was in serious danger of becoming overrun, but the vast numbers did have the effect of driving any locals and the Tunisian lads back where they had come from.

And so to the game the whole world was waiting to see: not Brazil v. Holland, not England v. Germany, but Iran v. the USA. If anyone ever tells you again that politics and football don't mix, then remind them of the effect this game had on the imagination of the whole world. The Yanks were desperate to play the whole thing down but a quote from the USA goalie Kasey Keller summed up what the rest were expecting to see: 'When you have played at Millwall and seen some of the things that go on there, this should be nothing I can't handle.'

Meanwhile, the French authorities were trying to keep the Iranians quiet and as far away as possible. It was reported on the television that 7,000 police were on duty and that the stadium security cordon had become tighter than a gnat's chuff. Border check points had stopped over 1,000 Iranians from entering the country, despite the fact that they were shown waving match tickets, which, considering the authorities had let hundreds of neo-Nazis slip by earlier in the day, seemed to be quite an achievement. Obviously spotting a little dusty bloke with jet-black hair and a moustache is written into the CRS training manual, whereas a tall, blond-haired lad in jackboots, happily goose-stepping by in the background, is a chapter someone unfortunately forgot to write. What a strange world this is!

Just like the first game of the day, this was an absolute blinder. The shrill whistling from the Iranian fans could never be totally drowned out by the director back in the television studio, although you could feel his desire to keep the cameras away from the section of the stadium where the majority of the Iranian fans were positioned. The 2–1 victory for the Iranians was greeted like no other, and you were left in no doubt that this was their World Cup final, and they had won all right. The result led to unprecedented scenes of joy on the streets of Tehran, and why not? 'The Great Satan' had been defeated. 'Tonight, once again, the strong and arrogant opponent felt the bitter taste of defeat', spouted one Iranian presenter. Personally, I was filled with a very strange emotion. For some reason I had really wanted Iran to win this match – underdogs and all that – but on seeing the way they celebrated I suddenly became very jealous. For a short, uncontrollable second I began to hope that, despite all their friendliness beforehand, the result would spark the Americans into direct action of the Exocet kind. Nothing too serious, of course; just the odd chemical warfare plant going up in smoke.

Once again we found ourselves wandering across the main square, aimlessly taking in the occasion, when suddenly in front of me I saw Wiltshire surrounded by a group of blokes and being led away. As I watched from a distance I could see them questioning him before making him stand against the wall and taking his photograph. Some fifteen minutes later they let him walk away, and I followed at a distance for a while before catching up with him. They were undercover English police and had pulled him because they said he had been seen causing trouble in Marseille. They had asked for his personal details and telephoned his local police station to check them out. One of the officers, a black guy who I believe works on all the England away games, also questioned Wiltshire about an incident that happened the last time England played in Poland, but again, nothing came of that either.

The problem with this kind of police action is that everyone suddenly goes on the defensive; everyone's suddenly a suspect. Wiltshire's photograph would now appear on a register of so-called 'suspected hooligans' known by the police to have been in France. They originally pulled him under the guise of causing trouble in Marseille, which, it turned out, was total bollocks: if they had had any evidence of such violence he would have been dragged away there and then. For the football fan there is no comeback on policing such as this. You have no access to the register and there is no way of finding out what information the police have listed on you, whether it be fact or complete fiction. There are many people on the register at Scotland Yard who know nothing about fighting at football and wouldn't want to; they don't even know about the register, or that their mugshot is held upon it. Their only crime was that they walked past a police unit with a video camera while innocently on their way to watch the sport they love. Criminal, isn't it?

The police make a big play in the press back home of these newly arrived 'spotter squads' in Toulouse. They make a big play of the 'Football Intelligence Unit' and their register of known hooligans, giving them Categories A, B or C according to their violent history, or lack of it. Yet they fail to hold their heads quite so high when events get a little out of hand. To what use was all that information put in Marseille? Didn't it all go off back there? How many of those 'known faces' were arrested? And just what the fuck were the police actually doing? The tactic of coming onto the streets and pulling people over just doesn't work. It's nothing but show. Once one person has been tugged the word spreads like the rash you would get up the red light district. The hard core take to the back streets, the small cafés, restaurants and bars, so all the police succeed in doing is to spread the problem over a larger area. Coming to Toulouse was too little too late: the damage had already been done. By the time the plod arrived the hard core had already accomplished what they had set out to achieve.

Back in the Belgian bar the English abroad party was in full swing as I came across a group of blokes going for it at a hundred miles an hour. All of them were English but now lived in Australia, and they had seen France '98 as the perfect opportunity to head back to Europe. Two of them owned a night club in Sydney, and after just a few short moments one of them unfolded a small paper wrap and asked if I would like to indulge in a line of the white stuff. After refusing the offer they told me that between the lot of them they had been shafted for over £20,000 after package deals which included match tickets went belly up. They had still made their own way over but had told the lad that had arranged it for them that the money had better be there when they got back, or his legs would very quickly be removed from his body.

These blokes were obviously seriously loaded, and whereas I had found four days in Toulouse to be a little tedious, they had been having the time of their lives. They couldn't believe I hadn't found any of the strip bars or late-night drinking dens, and went on to explain that they had visited every whore house the city had to offer. In their wired state they asked me whether I fancied tagging along for the ride, but something told me that I didn't even want to shake their hands, let alone watch them ride.

The England lads across the road in the Melting Pot had once again managed to block off the main throughway, which prompted the arrival of the riot police. Whether they had been put on edge by the events at the Germany game in Lens or not I don't know, but their mood soon suggested to us that we'd be better off moving somewhere else and keeping out of their way.

We headed back towards the main square where I bumped into another fellow Watford fan and a good friend of mine, Pete. After the initial shock had passed, he went on to tell me that another Watford lad known to both of us had had his photograph splashed over the front pages of the national newspapers back home, branded as one of the most notorious football thugs England had to offer. The news both shocked and disappointed me at the same time.

If the lad in question has a middle name it certainly isn't 'lucky', as every move he makes comes under the microscope of those that currently run the club at Vicarage Road. He is so passionate about the game that his actions often lead to him being misunderstood by those that watch from a distance. Like many, he believes you should be able to sing at football, that you should be able to stand up, and that if a player isn't performing then he deserves to be told by those that pay his wages. A clash of personalities with people at the club who have been there for a fair few years less than he has led to the police hounding this lad wherever he went. Furthermore, on seeing the pictures in the newspaper I realised someone had fed the press more information so as to bury my friend. Indeed the informant in question hadn't seen or been anywhere near him when those pictures were taken; I'm not even sure he was at this tournament. I often wonder how such people can sleep at night.

The whole incident involving my friend blew up out of the same picture printed in the *Mirror* paper that had the false caption accusing an English fan of giving the Nazi salute. In the background of that picture there was a lad wearing a plastic bowler hat given to him by the *Sun* newspaper, and perhaps that is where the true angle on his victimisation by the press lies. Despite the fact that the lad in question was pictured doing absolutely nothing more than walking past smiling, the *Mirror* took it upon themselves to use him and the hat he was wearing to have a dig at the readers of their rivals.

The editor of the *Mirror* placed a picture of my friend on the front pages of his paper, a picture cropped so close that all you could see were his face and the hat worn by this shameful reader of the rival paper. It was a cheap dig that in two days' time probably meant nothing to them, yet my friend lost his livelihood. What happened to him was outrageous. It could have been any one of hundreds wearing that particular plastic give-away that afternoon, so the next time the *Mirror* or any other newspaper offers you a freebie I would think twice. You never know, there might be a photographer ready to accuse you of giving a Nazi salute, when in truth you are probably just pointing someone in the direction of the nearest toilet.

Pete, my mate who had first told me about this unsavoury incident, had only just arrived in Toulouse, but his journey had provided him with a few interesting moments:

I had missed out on Euro '96 mainly due to a rather tasty bit of class from Surbiton. I really wanted that relationship to last, but it didn't and I missed out, although I did get to see the 4–1 win over Holland from a rather unique position! Another time maybe. With visions of Marseille still firmly imprinted on my mind I left for France with a rumbling of fear, but arrived in Paris to find not row after row of riot police but happy people, smiling people.

I boarded my train south with the case full of duty free and no food. Bad mistake. I mean, where in the civilised world would you find a train that travels for about ten hours with no refreshments? The land of surrender and capitulation, of course. Sitting opposite me was a Gooner, a nice gentle-looking bloke, the kind you would expect to see at a Woking v. Arsenal Juniors pre-season match. He told me he had gone to Marseille and been chased up the road by a lad brandishing a Samurai sword. He laid the blame fairly and squarely with the North Africans – certainly not the English he was with. He thought he was going to get killed, yet here he was travelling out again, only this time he was steering well clear of the city until the day of the game. Now he was heading for Andorra after hearing a rumour about a secret warm-up match.

Next to join the table was Dan. He had wanted a beer,

and ended up having eight. In return he allowed me the use of his hotel room floor for the night, and he turned out to be a top lad. Dan was a Spurs fan from Stevenage and was out helping his friends tout tickets. His 'friends' had turned up just three hours after his girlfriend had left for work and offered him the trip of a lifetime; by the time she had returned from work he had crossed the Channel and hadn't been home since. All that happened nearly two weeks ago. He went on to tell me that while trying to hunt out England tickets in Paris he had been driven out into the countryside where he thought he was going to get shagged, killed or both. He came back with no tickets but an eighth of wacky-baccy. Dan went on to explain about the Japs being the best targets as they had been sold short on tickets and some were even sleeping in the stations in order to save as much money as possible. When we arrived in Toulouse we found that his hotel was right opposite the station, and at five a.m. I finally managed to get some sleep.

We were woken early by Dan's mates, ready and waiting to go off in search of tickets. To my amazement Dan let me stay in the room, offered me the floor for another night and felt comfortable enough to leave all his belongings with only me for company.

By the time I ventured out onto the streets the day was well underway. Everywhere I looked the English were just sitting around, chilling out and soaking up the sun. The main square was full of half-naked bodies, footballs and lads holding pieces of card that requested tickets. These people were full of hope, football fans who had travelled hundreds of miles in support of their country. This wasn't the image of the English football fan being shown back in England.

As I roamed around proudly displaying the team shirt of my league club, I suddenly came across two so-called fans of the scum, the enemy. They slagged me, I returned the insults, then we began to talk. From somewhere we had found the common ground that was England away. Here I was talking to two of them and it was OK! We both commented on what our mates would say, then disaster struck as Chris Scudder from Sky News appeared and began to interview us. We all tried to stop but it was too late – the pictures of us together were already in the can, there to haunt us for ever. All three of us mortified.

With the sun sinking, a game of football began to engulf the main square. At first it was England v. France, camera crews looking on for the trouble to start. Then at 11–0 the game turned into a scrum more suited to the Eton Wall than an international friendly. I witnessed a Portsmouth fan put in a very late tackle on a 'comrade' from Southampton, but I am sure he never meant it! This was what we wanted. I was floating. Was I at a world football love-in, or maybe it was just the beer taking over!

While getting in a goodnight snack on the way back to the hotel we bumped into a Tottenham fan who had just been released by the Old Bill from the local nick, something that explained his broad smile. He had got lifted while being offered a ticket up at the train station for £300. He had given the lad £80, snatched the ticket and then done the off. The lad he had relieved it from chased after him, and unfortunately the police had seen them both running and joined in the chase. When the police heard both stories they made the two of them swap the ticket and the money before dragging him off and banging him up for a few hours. The French lad was just sent packing. So much for the crackdown on ticket touting.

All the time he was locked up they had wound him up about sending him back home as soon as they could get him on a train, so despite his ordeal he was well chuffed at being let off without charge. While in the cell he had picked up on a rumour that the police were expecting over 1,500 spare Romanian tickets to be arriving in the city tomorrow, so when we left him our hopes of actually getting to see the game were high.

At two a.m. Pete headed back to his room, a room he later found out contained an additional seven bodies and the smells that go with them.

As I climbed into bed I realised that by this time tomorrow I would be well and truly on my way back to England. Roll on tomorrow.

Living Out The Dream – Well, Almost
Day 13: Monday, 22 June

Wiltshire and I woke early and made our way down the stairs in order to have breakfast. As we entered, the room fell silent and all eyes fixed upon us. Immediately we realised that we had walked into a room full of journalists, and you could feel them desperately trying to pluck up the courage to ask us 'typical English lads' for an interview. Wiltshire and I sat, not even talking to each other, and listened in as they began to pass on the rumours they had heard from the day before. A well-known female journalist then walked into the room and sparked up the type of conversation that had me wanting to suddenly butt in and tell her to shut the fuck up. She started with the line, 'Well, that was like a mini Marseille last night up at the Melting Pot, wasn't it!'

To be fair, another of her fellow workmates answered back: 'Why, did something happen late on? I didn't see anything.'

'Well, nothing really happened, but the riot police were just waiting for it. All the English lads were blocking the road and it was looking very nasty at one stage. I was expecting trouble any moment.'

'Oh right. But it didn't?' Short pause. 'Surely, then, the story should be there wasn't any trouble?'

Wiltshire and I sat back and waited as the discussion unfolded. The embarrassing silence was broken as she dodged the question and offered up a total gem.

'We've found out there are some run-down areas of the city where all the Africans and Arabs live. We're going out there today to film what they think of the English hooligans.'

And the press honestly wonder why they have suddenly become the target of so many attacks themselves! I ask you.

The first objective today was to get packed, settle the bill and then head for the station in order to secure our bags in the train station luggage room before all the lockers got taken. This was the last day of the first part of my France '98 trip; after tonight's match it would be a mad dash back to the station to catch the 12.35 a.m. train back to Paris. Our next priority was to get out onto the streets and ask anyone who passed by whether or not they had a ticket to sell.

Although it was still early morning, the number of English on the streets had increased fivefold as those on the overnight trains had swelled the numbers. We headed straight for the main square and were greeted by a sight that would fill any Englishman with pride. The walls of the town hall had been dressed in flags bearing the names of just about every English town you could imagine. One of the first I managed to pick out was that of Herne Bay, and within seconds we were re-united with the man who had shared the room with us on the first night. Once again he was having the time of his life and was able to relax, safe in the knowledge that he already had a ticket tucked away in his back pocket. For us the search went on, and as the England fans continued to grow in number I became increasingly worried. I really wanted to see this game as I was sure that I wouldn't have a chance of seeing England play Colombia in Lens – every lad in the country was planning to make that trip.

While we continued our search another face from the past came into view as we spotted J. the ticket tout going about his business. In his hand he had a sheet of cardboard and was moonlighting by selling England badges. It was good to see that he was all right and he told us that the Argentinian fans had played up in Paris the night before with both the locals and the French riot police. He too was finding tickets hard to come by, hence the badge selling, but had managed to recoup some of his cash on his trip to Nantes, thanks to the naivety of the Japanese.

As the English fans poured into the main square the vibe became better and better. Even some of the camera crews picked up on the fact that the violence they had expected, and in some cases wanted, just wasn't going to happen. The Romanian fans mixed happily with us as congas and football matches sprung up all over the place, the sound of 'Ing-ger-land' and 'Rule Britannia' filling the air. Then my eyes fell on a most beautiful sight. The main square of Toulouse is massive, but only one car managed to get itself parked up on the pedestrianised area without getting towed away. That car was draped in a Cross of Saint George with a huge Harry Hornet, the Watford FC mascot, embroidered upon it. It was enough to make my heart weep. Following England is special, but I have to say that for me my club is in many ways even more important.

The police had handled the day really well, an obvious result of the previous night's good behaviour. Although their presence was there for all to see they mostly kept themselves tucked away down the side streets so as not to be seen as heavy-handed. They also issued a notice that the square would be emptied, and that all flags were to be taken down at six o'clock. When that time came I saw no one complaining as everyone knew what to expect and what was going on, a little forward thinking going a long way.

The time had come to move off in the direction of the stadium and step up the search for a ticket. As we made our way through the cobbled back streets we passed many locals out with their one ticket to sell. I shall never forget the sight of one child out with his mum holding up a piece of card with the words 'I have one ticket for £300' written upon it. The words 'taking', 'candy' and 'baby' did cross my mind, yes, but as his mother looked a bit of a bruiser I walked swiftly by.

We were then given a stark warning as to what might happen if everything turned nasty. Into view came a French riot cop and his dog, both of them looking like they had just stepped off the film set of *Mad Max*. The copper was built like a brick shit house, and his dog, a Rottweiler, was trussed up in leather straps that were covered with metal studs. I have never been a great lover of dogs since the use of one upon my person by the Hertfordshire police force many years ago, and this one wasn't going to change my mind.

We arrived at the ground early, but to my disappointment our chosen path had taken us to the opposite side of the island to the one where all the buses arrive. I had felt all along that my best chance of getting a ticket would have been where the buses drop people off, as that was where all the tickets were being sold before the Denmark game, yet here I was on the other side of the river. In order to get that side of the island I would have to walk back to the main square and then out again. On this side things were way too quiet for my liking, and as every minute passed I became more and more agitated. Parked up along the side of the river bank I could see all the corporate coaches, and in the hotel opposite the money men and sponsors were entertaining their guests. As we sat on the side of the road we could see and hear those inside getting drunk and singing the songs they never quite knew the right words to, which had the effect of making me feel as though I was having my nose well and truly rubbed in the dirt.

Small groups of locals were now starting to appear, ready to unload their tickets on the many England fans milling around. On this side of the bridge the police once again seemed uninterested in the free enterprise going on around them, but as Sharon from Gillingham later told me, it was a different story on the other side of the river bank:

Again we travelled there and back to this game, using an overnight train which was packed with England fans. We had given up on looking for a ticket during the day and decided on waiting until the last minute like every-one else in the hope that the price would fall. It was so annoying seeing all the locals walking around with their one ticket. To go all that way and see that is such a wind-up.

There were ten of us in the end, five from the Medway and five West Bromwich Albion fans we had met during the day. Not long after we got to the ground we spotted a couple of French lads selling tickets and straight away one of these WBA fans snatched one out of their hands. These local lads went mental and everyone started pushing and telling them to fuck off. I got the Brummie lad to give me the ticket and then I stuffed it down the side of my trainer and moved away. Then these French lads went off and we thought that was it, but five minutes later they turned up with the police. We couldn't believe it. All they said about ticket touting and these bastards not only had the nerve to run and tell the police but the police were willing to get their tickets back for them. It all started to look really nasty with the police getting heavy and these French ponces pointing and shouting. Then out of nowhere a man appeared representing the Football Association. First he started talking to the police, then began asking us what was going on and told my mate Richard to get his ticket out for the police to look at. Richard told the bloke to fuck off and said he wasn't getting his ticket out for no one. We then all started having a go at this FA bloke because it was down to him and that lot that we were shafted for tickets in the first place. Richard told him to piss off and mind his own business because the FA had done fuck all for us in the past and here he was coming down on the side of the French when they were trying to rip us off. After hearing all that he just threw his arms up and said, 'Fuck you then, you're on your own', and walked off. Wanker.

Once he had gone the police got really heavy with this West Bromwich lad, so I got the ticket back out and handed it back to the French guy. Then the police gave us some kind of warning and told us to piss off somewhere else. Thankfully we did all manage to get tickets in the end for £125, but the way the police protected those lads was out of order.

With little over an hour to kick-off some lads on my side of the river were also beginning to think about turning the locals over rather than pay the £200 asking price. I had said all along that I would never pay more than £150 for a ticket, so I looked on with interest as rumours spread. Then suddenly my world took a major turn for the better as I heard Wiltshire say the bloke next to him had a ticket but was asking too much for it.

The man had just come from the hotel opposite and was part of one of the promotional groups. He was about 45 years old, stocky build and wearing a shirt and tie that had the English Football Association emblem stitched upon it. For some reason no one else seemed to want to take him up on his offer, but when he told me that he wanted just £125 for it I nearly ripped his hand off. He went on to explain that the ticket also included a meal at a hospitality function once the game was over and had included drinks beforehand, although by now that freebie had passed. He went on to spin some unlikely story about the ticket belonging to his mate who for some reason had been locked in the coach park and was unable to get out, but at this point I didn't give a toss where the thing had come from. All I wanted to know was whether it was the real deal or not. A quick hold-up to the heavens confirmed the watermark, so £125 rapidly headed his way.

I soon left the others behind and made my way to the first police check point. As every step drew me closer my brain reminded me of the advertising campaign fronted by the English Football Association that told me I wouldn't get near the stadium with a ticket that had a French name upon it. A quick check on the ticket confirmed to me the name M. Coustilleres and my stomach tightened. I needn't have worried, passing through without even getting looked at. The next step was to get through what looked like the official stadium turnstiles. Once again, the ticket drew no real attention as a quick body search seemed far more important to those there to welcome me.

Living Out The Dream – Well, Almost

Suddenly the realisation hit home that I had actually made it into the stadium. Not more than five minutes ago I was in panic at the thought of missing yet another England game, yet now I found myself safely past the first two check points with just 45 minutes to go before kick-off. Here, within the stadium fences, France '98 took on a completely different feel as street entertainers, musicians and supporters mingled together in a relaxed and happy atmosphere. A quick walk around the stadium confirmed to me that my seat was one of the best in the house, just to the side of the halfway line and midway up the stand. I also woke up to the fact that as my ticket came as part of a corporate package it was likely that the people I would be sitting with would be well dressed, suited and booted, while unfortunately I wasn't. I quickly remembered the story of the Birmingham lad who had been arrested with the corporate ticket at Marseille, and once again panic set in. Fortunately, during the day I had purchased a cheap France '98 T-shirt as a memento, so I quickly swapped it with the top I had been wearing in an attempt to look a little less laddish. I took one last long, deep breath, then headed off to Porte 21 of the Stade Municipal, Toulouse.

To my utter delight I was greeted with a happy smile and told to enjoy the game, no questions asked. The sight that welcomed me took my breath away. The official allocation for the England fans was meant to be no more than 8,000 tickets, yet apart from a small corner that housed approximately 1,500 Romanians the whole ground was covered in England red, white and blue. The sound of *The Great Escape* theme tune rang out loud and clear as what appeared to be around 25,000 English men and women sang their hearts out. I had made it. One of my lifetime ambitions was taking place right before my eyes. No matter what those that run the game had told me, I was here to see England kick off a game in the World Cup finals, along with about 17,000 others who had been told to stay at home.

The support the England team received that night was relentless. As expected, I found myself in a section full of

French people and suities, but I joined in with the singing for all I was worth. As the minutes ticked by the locals slowly began to realise that despite all they had seen and heard about the English we knew as well as anyone how to have a good time, and soon they too warmed to the occasion. The start of the second 45 minutes brought disaster as far as the English were concerned, Moldovan putting the Romanians 1–0 ahead. I could see the look of anxiety flash across the faces of all those around me as they waited for the English reaction to the goal, but their worries were short-lived as we responded in song rather than with violence. The arrival on the pitch of substitute Michael Owen brought new hope as the result seemed to be slipping away. Then, with just seven minutes left, the new hero of English football set the stadium alight by planting the ball firmly in the back of the net.

These are the moments all football fans live for. The golden moments that make all the crap worth it. I swear I rose six feet off the ground as every bone in my body sprung into action. My fist punched the air faster than a Prince Naseem right hook and I hugged the bloke next to me like a long-lost brother whom I had just met for the first time in 20 years. They must have been able to hear the noise back home in England, as for the next six minutes every England fan played their part in lifting the roof. The atmosphere was electrifying, and I really believe that at that moment even the French people around me began to want England to win. Honest!

As we gave it our all, urging the boys forward towards that winning goal, the unthinkable happened. The Romanians broke forward, Graeme Le Saux got roasted and Petrescu slotted the ball between Seaman's legs to put them 2–1 ahead to steal a famous victory. The yellow, red and blue flags of the Romanian fans were raised as one and began waving from side to side in a colourful frenzy while the English looked on in disbelief. 'No! No! That wasn't meant to happen!'

The final whistle blew and the mad dash for the station quickly began. It wasn't until I was firmly seated on the Metro that the result finally hit home. Everything had gone well and truly tits-up as far as the England team was concerned as now the possibility of winning the group had seriously slipped away.

As I listened to the comments of those around me all I could hear were words of disappointment. Some were disgusted with the way England had played and bitterly angry at coming all this way to watch such a poor game, but as far as I was concerned I wouldn't have missed it for the world. I was a fan, and we had played our part. The atmosphere in that ground was like no other I had ever experienced; my voice was hoarse and I felt physically and emotionally drained. It didn't really matter to me that the team had lost because we the fans had done all we could to spur the side on, and in the process of doing so had let the rest of the world know that we were the most loyal and passionate on this planet.

Of course, while 99.9 per cent of English fans were wallowing in the pain of defeat, our friends north of the border were slightly less bothered by the result, as Tom wrote to tell me:

Oh yes! Oh yes yes yes yes yes! To see the look on the faces of you English bastards when that second goal went in. Truly wonderful. I have recorded the match just to see those pictures over and over. In my moments of pain I can reach for instant relief. Thank you. I've already applied to take in a Romanian orphan just so as to have an excuse to watch it all again and have someone to share it with. For once it all went against you, everything: hitting the post, bad goals conceded. And it was a player in your own overrated league that got the winner, as well as the first one. The English think they are so good, so special, oh so talented. Well, you were shite that night and up here it was greeted by the majority rather than the minority.

They're coming home, they're coming, England's coming home. Be seeing you.

Meanwhile, my friend Pete had left Toulouse before the match and headed off to Bordeaux for a rather different experience:

In the cold light of day I wasn't that sorry to leave Toulouse. I knew before I set off that I was never going to get a ticket, so that is why I had arranged to meet my mate Rup in Bordeaux, away from the hassle and the ticket touts.

The first thing that struck me about this city was not the dry heat but the amount of porn everywhere. Now I am fairly permissive, I like the odd bit of in and out, but the amount of sickness that greeted me as I left the station was a bit over the top. I know it's legal, but it shouldn't be presented as part of the scenery.

After checking into the hotel it was time to track down Rup, a man not known ever to be in a hurry. To my horror I discovered that he had booked himself on a train due to arrive at 8.53 p.m., the match kicking off at nine. Idiot! I set off to kill the time until Rup's arrival and soon found that I was not alone in my decision to travel here for the match. In a small bar I met up with lads from Leeds and Hull before we were joined by four South African supporters over in France for the whole month. It turned out that two of them were actually from Scotland but had headed south over twenty years ago, there reasoning: 'Scotland is shit, so we went and became millionaires somewhere warm.' Fair comment really.

I've always hated Scotland when it comes to sport. This myth that all the English want jolly old Scotland to do well is a joke. We want them to lose, and lose badly! They hate us, so what is wrong for us, as their superiors, to hate them? And the different media perception of us compared to them is outrageous. Out of all the thousands of English that travel abroad, how many actually do get involved in trouble? It's a tiny minority. Meanwhile, the Scots see exposing themselves and showing their arses as a national greeting, yet no one says a word. If the English were to walk the streets as pissed up as the Scottish they would all be arrested and shipped home.

We were then joined by some Moan United fans, both English lads but following Scotland! What is the world coming to? They went on about not getting tickets and just wanting to see some football, which beggars the question 'Why Scotland?' Then they started on about all the English fans hating Moan Utd. They were going on about club rivalries, saying that England fans have a go at Beckham and Sheringham only because they play for the biggest team in the world. But the Scots were different, they said; all that club rivalry goes out the window as they believe they are all playing for their country. What a couple of tossers. I don't see too many Rangers and Celtic fans walking along hand in hand, or Aberdeen and Dundee supporters buying each other drinks!

As the day wore on and the drink flowed we all found common ground about the country of our birth. We all agreed that we had gone way too far down the road of political correctness. We can't call a woman a bird, you can't sing 'Jerusalem' or 'Rule Britannia' without being branded this or that, but you can ring your local council office and get asked the same question in five different languages!

At seven minutes to nine I meet Rup at the station. I am pissed, he is strolling. AHHHH. Following some stiff words and a swift taxi ride we find ourselves at the big screen beside the river where the Scots are rolling around in their own piss with their dicks hanging out of their dresses like ceremonial swords! And the locals think it's good clean fun!

As the game wears on the drink flows freely. The Scots do their best to out-sing us while the French don't know who to support as the game goes 0–1, 1–1, 1–2 Romania. SHIT, SHIT, SHIT! More penis shaking from the Jocks, no sound from us. I am fucked, fucked off and pissed. I have drunk myself stupid and sung myself hoarse for a team that is shit! Still, I imagine it was better than standing outside the stadium in Toulouse, gutted at not being able to find that golden ticket!

Meanwhile, I arrived back at the station to find Mr B already waiting. Suddenly Tony and Wiltshire appeared, both looking more than a little worse for wear. Neither of them had managed to get a ticket for the game and had watched it in a bar, becoming increasingly pissed by the minute. However, once they had seen people beginning to leave the ground they had run back and managed to steam into the stadium along with a few hundred others. Unfortunately they arrived just in time to catch the last five minutes.

For the first time the French appeared to be on the case as far as checking out the train tickets was concerned. With the aid of the heavy police presence this was going to pose problems as Mr B and Tony were booked on another train while Wiltshire never even had a ticket to start with. As we made our way up the stairs we decided to bundle our way through with me showing my reserved seat ticket in order to distract the ticket inspector. As Tony pushed his way through one of the platform masters went after him, allowing Wiltshire and Mr B to sneak by. With Tony's attitude and general drunken air ensuring that the platform master couldn't be fucked, we once again managed to board a train without using a day's travel on our passes, or in Wiltshire's case using a franc note from his wallet.

By this stage I was completely knackered, so I left the lads to find the buffet car while I went off in search of my comfy seat. After an hour or so of battling for leg room with some lanky Northampton fan I gave up the fight and found myself a sleeping space underneath a luggage rack, where for the next four hours I was kept awake by the sound of flushing toilets and people kicking my head. Oh, the joys of international travel by train!

As we headed north I heard that one England fan was seriously ill in hospital after being stabbed in the stomach. The British press reported this incident as if it were an afterthought, tacked on as the last paragraph. I wonder what they would have made of it if the victim had been a local rather than an Englishman?

156

Hello The Wife, Bye Bye The Jocks
Day 14: Tuesday, 23 June

I was shocked to be woken by the sound of feet stomping past my head as they made their way from the TGV train and onto the platform of Paris Montparnasse station. The sudden jolt made me bang my head on the metal rails above, much to the delight of some of my fellow travellers.

I grabbed my bag and jumped off the train to be greeted by the worrying sight of row upon row of French riot police waiting to guide us down onto the Metro and across the city to the Gare du Nord station. They stood with their guns across their chests forming a long tunnel from which there appeared no escape, and at six o'clock in the morning their heavy presence took on an added edge as anyone trying to break free from the escort was told firmly to get back and join the procession.

Rumours then began to spread that trouble had flared up in Toulouse late last night after the game, and that was the reason for this rather hostile greeting in Paris. On hearing the news I immediately felt gutted as the people in that city had, in the end, made us welcome. Once again the feeling of being ashamed to be English washed over me, and all I wanted now was to get on the Eurostar and leave France well and truly behind me.

As I made my way through the network of tunnels I soon

came across the others, who looked even worse than they had before. Wiltshire was in a particularly bad way with Tony looking none too attractive either, but this time it wasn't the drink that had them flaking out. Both of them had been up all night talking to a journalist from a well-known men's magazine, a journalist known for writing about the use of illegal drugs. Their main topics of conversation through the night had been football, birds, the art of drinking and, as befitted this journalist, drug-taking. Wiltshire was in serious danger of losing the plot and went on to explain that he felt the aforementioned journalist had spiked his drink, and he was tripping his nuts off. A quick look into his eyes seemed to add weight to his fears as his pupils were the size of dinner plates. Mr B and I did our best to keep them both straight, get them safely on the Metro and away from the prying eyes of the police.

We arrived at the Gare du Nord with just half an hour to spare before the Eurostar I had booked was due to depart, so now it was time for me to say goodbye to Mr B, Tony and Wiltshire. Although I was desperate to get home, this moment was tinged with sadness, for me anyway. Over the last ten days there had been many moments when I wanted to kill each and every one of them, but I was also in no doubt that there had been many, many more occasions when they had either helped me out of a dodgy situation or had me cracking up laughing. I am sure they had wanted to kill me at times too, especially Tony, but for some reason we had been thrown together and, more remarkably, we had all managed to come through unscathed – well, kind of. Before saying our final goodbyes we all agreed that we would try to meet up at the next game in Lens on Friday, and then I was gone up the escalator.

I still couldn't believe that in a little over three hours' time I would be back in London and drinking a proper cup of tea. I never wanted to see another croissant again, and if someone were to offer me a baguette at Euston then I swore to myself there and then I would stick the offending snack so far up his arse that it would be pushing against his tonsils. I even began to think about showing the Great British bobby a little more respect in the future, but soon realised that lack of sleep must have had me hallucinating, so I kicked such thoughts into touch.

Once on the Eurostar my lack of personal hygiene following on from the previous night's sleeping arrangements ensured that I had more than my fair share of allocated seats in which to stretch out. The businessmen and women on their way to London giving me a wide, wide berth. Within seconds I was dead to the world as the land of nod came to visit, and three hours later I was woken up, at arm's length, by the lovely hostess just as the train arrived in Waterloo. Following a short tube journey across London I found myself at Euston and talking to a friend of mine who works the station as a ticket collector. He told me that there had been very little on the news about trouble in Toulouse, and I soon found out that the rumour about serious trouble flaring up after the game was in fact total and utter bullshit. It goes to show that one prat can make an idiotic comment that has the effect of putting every-one around them on edge and believing the worst. I couldn't help thinking that the person who started it would make one hell of a journalist.

I finally arrived home to find the wife open-armed with tears running down her face. She too had returned from holiday only to find a string of messages concerned about my well-being. She had now seen the news footage, read the papers and heard all the tales, and couldn't believe that her little soldier had returned from Armageddon with his life and all his limbs intact. I spent the rest of the day having to ring family and friends in order to reassure people I was alive, functioning properly and actually all right. The stories they were relaying back about what they had seen on the news had me thinking I must have been in another part of the planet altogether. This was my first indication of just how bad the media had played it back home. I spent much of the day pawing through the backlog of papers and wondering just how the English press can honestly live with themselves.

Coming home was strange. France, the World Cup, the football on the telly, it all seemed a million miles away. Reading the papers was like living through some surreal dream, the events I had witnessed with my own eyes being described in a totally different way.

That afternoon I watch the luck finally run out for those kings of seventies fashion, the Austrians. This band of Abba fan club look-a-likes score yet again in the last minute, but by that time Italy are already two goals to the good and the match finishes 2–1 to the pizza chompers. Chile also qualify thanks to a very dubious 1–1 draw with Cameroon, the Africans more than a little hard done by following some very iffy refereeing decisions. Cameroon have a clear goal disallowed, miss a sitter in added time, and despite finishing the match with just nine men really should have won. The referee's decisions cause quite a stir back home as angry Cameroon supporters attack businesses owned by white expatriates as they believe the result reflected some anti-African plot hatched by World Cup officials!

That night we come to the game all Scotland has been waiting for. This is to be the night when they finally secure themselves that elusive place in the second round of the World Cup, and prove to us all that they are no longer mere whipping boys. It's not that surprising, then, when the plan falls apart. The Scottish players never once appear to get out of second gear as the Moroccans take them apart, winning 3–0. The pictures shown later that night on the news of distraught Scots in the bars north of the border should be enough to make every Englishman's heart leap with joy, but personally I could only allow myself a short burst of laughter. I actually like 99 per cent of the Scots I've ever met, and I think the same could be said for most English people. I don't think it's unfortunate that sport has us clashing head to head – it shows passion – but away from that I have many good Scottish friends. I know how much their football means to them. I know a few who travelled to France, spent their hard-earned wages and used up all their holiday. For them this was a big chance, yet the display put forward by a team chosen to represent them even has me, a full-blooded Englishman, looking on in disgust rather than gloating. I actually feel sorry for Scottish football tonight, although it is still highly amusing. Some of the players even appear on television and admit that, yes, they are disappointed, but as they had never really expected to qualify from such a strong group in the first place, it isn't unexpected! Just what a supporter wants to hear!

As the Moroccans celebrate what they assume to be qualification for the next phase, the unthinkable is happening down in Marseille where Norway are diving their way to victory over Brazil. The 2–1 win for the Scandinavians, secured by an outrageous penalty decision in the last minute, means that Norway leap-frog the Africans into second spot. The standard of the match officials later has the chairman of African football, Issa Hayatou, complaining to FIFA, but by then both Cameroon and Morocco are on their way home.

Penalty, Ref! Oh, All Right Then
Day 15: Wednesday, 24 June

Today the refereeing reaches new lows as penalties are given out left, right and centre. France secure maximum points from their group games with a 2–1 win over Denmark, who also qualify, and suddenly we get the feeling that the French people might just start to warm to this football tournament type thingy that has been dumped upon them. The two no-hopers in this group, South Africa and Saudi Arabia, draw 2–2.

Later that night Spain finally come alive, scoring six against the abysmal Bulgarians who offer only one in reply. Spain manage to finish as second-highest scorers in the group stages, but the surprise 3–1 win by Paraguay over Nigeria also has the Spanish heading home. The television coverage of both matches is excellent as we flick from one stadium to the next. One minute we see flashes of delighted Central Americans, the next tearful Spaniards. Brilliant. The joyous goalkeeper Chilavert is quoted as saying, 'We have embarrassed teams who thought Paraguay were easy meat because we are a poor, small country with many of our people starving. But when we want something we get it.'

The BBC studio suddenly finds itself minus one replica World Cup trophy as their hired, rare and expensive visual prop goes missing. No one dares ask if it's not to be found firmly implanted up the backside of Jimmy Hill following yet another disagreement with Des and Alan.

Day 16: Thursday, 25 June

Today over 90 England fans are arrested following trouble in Ostend, Lille and Lens ahead of tomorrow's game. The papers are busy whipping up the storm and my family are doing their best to convince me to go down the pub with them rather than cross the Channel. Friend after friend telephones, only to tell me they want to drop out from the trip as they believe it's a waste of time, but in stubborn defiance I convince myself into going.

Today's football provides one of those special games as Holland take on Mexico. Again the Mexicans only start to play when 2–0 down, but a ninetieth-minute strike from Hernandez wins them a point from a 2–2 draw and sends the other group hopefuls, Belgium, on the short journey home, along with the joint hosts of the 2002 World Cup, South Korea. The South Koreans are unlucky, but Yoo's seventieth-minute goal earns them a point and sends them packing with a slice of pride as well.

Later that night the Iranians take on the ageing Germans with a new-found belief following their victory over the USA. Before the game, and following on from the trouble caused by the German fans in Lens, border police stop and check over 10,000 fans. Fourteen suspected hooligans are arrested and television news footage shows one car being relieved of its passengers, four knives, a hammer and a club. For long periods the Iranians look like causing the surprise result this World Cup requires, but eventually the knee slappers break through, score two in eight minutes and send the Iranians off to the barbers to have their facial hair trimmed. Yugoslavia round up the group by beating the Americans 1–0, leaving Team USA with no points and just one goal, a kick in the nuts for a country that is turning what was once known as football into 'soccer'. I fucking hate that word.

The day ends with the news that following their humiliating 6–1 defeat by Spain, the Bulgarian coach Hristo Bonev has resigned. But who gives a fuck?

Day 17: Friday, 26 June

Finally the day arrived to get back on the World Cup trail and shift myself back over to France. Since the second the draw had been made, this day had been billed 'The Great English Piss-up' as the venue for England's final group match lay just over 45 minutes' drive from the ferry port at Calais. Once again I found myself travelling alone as friend after friend backed out due to reports of extortionate ticket prices and the drink ban that had been imposed by the authorities upon the small northern mining town.

The press back home had refused to heed the warnings from the government, and in their own special way told anyone who wanted to believe them that the worst was about to happen all over again. This time the French, the Belgians and the Dutch were coming to town for the big off. Remember those Argentinian neo-Nazis? Well, they're coming too, as well as the Germans. And if aliens land then don't be surprised as this *is* the big one. The unfortunate thing is that people actually believe that shit. The Mayor of Lens, André Delelis, only added fuel to the fire by stating his support for the South Americans: 'It is only fair that Colombia win, because the English have shut down my town.'

Once again I had to spend hours convincing my wife that everything was going to be all right; hours getting my dad to ask himself if he really thought those German hooligans would return to a town where their faces would be instantly recognised; and hours settling arguments between my brothers as to who would get my TV and video rather than the mountain bike once my impending death had been confirmed. Personally, I couldn't believe how any self-respecting Englishman could even contemplate missing this one. I was 100 per cent certain that I would never get a ticket to see the game, but something inside told me that I just had to be there, I had to give it a go. So at 7.30 a.m. I found myself bombing around the M25 towards Kent and the coastal town of Dover, passing likeminded people bearing that same 'Lens or Bust' look in their eye.

Staring the Grim Reaper firmly between the eyes, my trip went ahead regardless. I was far more concerned with England actually winning the game, and I have to admit as the car trundled over the Queen Elizabeth II Bridge I was feeling more than a little pessimistic. On arriving at Dover ferry terminal I made a beeline straight towards the P&O Stena ticket desk, only to be told that all their vessels were fully booked and that no foot passengers were being taken on board until gone three o'clock. Around me were supporters from all over the country who had travelled hundreds of miles in order to be told the same bad news. As an air of depression filled the terminal it appeared that all our plans had been shot down in flames before we had even managed to leave the country. The late sailing time would make arriving in Lens in time for kickoff virtually impossible, so many of those around me resigned themselves to the fact that they'd be better off getting back in their cars and heading home in order to watch the game in their local.

Personally, I was having none of it and decided that the best course of action would be to hunt down someone in a car or lorry who was willing to let me sit in on their ticket in return for a few extra quid. Once I was the other side it didn't really matter as I would be able to travel freely without hassle from the authorities. It was just getting across the water that posed the immediate problem. After spending almost an hour asking anything that moved whether they had a spare seat or not, I came across another two lads from Leicester who had been busy playing the same game, only now they were both wearing a grin wider than a David Batty goal attempt. They told me to get myself over to the Sea France sailings desk as they had a ferry leaving in little over half an hour and had just started taking foot passenger bookings. Five minutes later I found myself what I thought to be a very reasonable £11 lighter, with a seat booked on the 12.25 p.m. out and a return sailing at 1.45 in the morning. Lovely job.

As the ferry pulled itself away from the dock I allowed myself time to relax before turning my mind back to the issue of finding a ticket. I soon began talking with two north London lads who, unbeknown to me, had been observing my activities from a distance back in the ferry terminal in order to pass the time. They told me that their original idea was to make a bet between themselves on the type of person I was before striking up conversation on the boat and finding out the truth. Unfortunately they had both come up with the same conclusion so all bets were off, but we had struck up enough of an understanding for them to inform me of the rather damning first impressions I was obviously giving out. They both felt that due to my shaved head, my shifty behaviour when approaching strangers and the fact I was travelling alone, I could only be a hard-core neo-Nazi who was desperately trying to get to France undetected, my obvious objective then being to hook up with my storm-trooping colleagues so that we could instigate as much violence as possible and once again drag the name of England through the gutter. That's nice of them, I thought. And there I was thinking I was dressed in my best togs. With a stereotypical thought process such as that I came to the conclusion that these two lads must either be journalists, detective superintendents or researchers for the *Kilroy* television programme, so I felt it best I leave them well alone so that they could pick on someone else instead of yours truly.

As expected, the boat was packed with England fans, 90

per cent of whom appeared to have no tickets. It was obvious that demand to see the match would heavily outweigh the supply of tickets, so the idea uppermost in the minds of the majority was that of getting totally rat-arsed so that they no longer remembered where or even why they had been travelling in the first place. As well as the drinks ban, rumours were circulating that as all the bars were to be closed there would be nowhere to watch the game on television either. As this was such an important game that too had me beginning to panic.

Whoever imposed the 24-hour drinks ban in France had obviously overlooked the option of extending those powers to the ferries. In all my days I have never seen a duty free shop relieved so rapidly of its stock, the tills drowning out the irritating sounds of the nearby arcade machines. At just past midday on a Friday afternoon it was laughable to see lads and lasses struggling to find space for their prize possession, and the looks on the faces of our continental cousins who found themselves caught up in the frenzy were a picture. Personally I wanted to stay sober and on the case, but Steve from Woking, who landed himself down on the floor next to me, summed up the general feeling quite nicely. He was travelling with his girlfriend and another three blokes and they were definitely out to have a good time no matter what:

> We've been planning this for months. This is our World Cup and a big weekend away all in one. We knew it was unlikely we'd get tickets, even before the tournament started, but we're out to have a great weekend and make the most of it. Before all the trouble started almost the whole of Woking was coming over for this one, but I think the drink ban and what happened with the German fans here has put most people off. We've got a camper van with a fridge for this lot, and a television that I hook up to the battery, so we definitely won't miss the game no matter what. We all said we'd pay up to £150 as this is the only game we were going to, but from what people

are saying we haven't got a chance at that price and so we might not even go to Lens and just head for a camp site somewhere instead. At the moment I ain't too bothered either way. No matter what happens we'll get totally pissed and finish this lot over the weekend, then hit the hypermarket on Sunday when we're on our way home. At least that way we can say we went to France for the World Cup.

By the time the ferry docked at Calais the best price I had heard for a ticket was £280, way out of my league. On disembarking I found myself along with fifty or so fellow foot passengers walking around aimlessly as the French once again managed to cock it up on the organisation front. With no shuttle buses to greet us we moved in all directions like lost sheep before some ten minutes later a stewardess came to our rescue and got on the blower to port control.

Ten more minutes passed before we eventually found ourselves on a bus heading off in the direction of the train station. As we twisted our way through the streets of Calais I couldn't help but observe the behaviour of my fellow countrymen, and I quickly came to the conclusion that if, God forbid, I were of any other nationality I too would be scared of the English. One particular group of youngsters from High Wycombe could have provided the world's media with enough fuel to last a lifetime as they abused the driver to his face, the locals through the window and the police from a distance. 'These fuckers should all speak English' seemed to be the general consensus, along with a hatred for all that is German and the obvious references to the war. It didn't matter to them that the nearest they had personally been to a gun was when they received a Power Rangers replica a few Christmases back; as far as they were concerned *they* had won the war and Froggy had better be grateful for the fact (hic). How did these lads honestly expect to get hold of a ticket while in such a state? To make the effort and to come all this way only to get that pissed is madness to me. To my cost I have learnt over the years that football and drink can turn out to be dodgy bedfellows, and if ever there were a game when a clear head was vitally important then surely the one we were all hoping to see today was it. The expectation of violence that surrounded this match, coupled with a police force already on edge, provided a power keg waiting to blow at any moment. Patience would be tested to its limit and fools quickly sent packing, and believe me, this bus was packed with fools.

When the bus finally came to a halt I was as pleased as the driver to find myself some space away from the knobheads. We were greeted by the sight of two riot vans full of uninterested policemen, while on the corner ahead of me I could see a small gathering of lads talking with two local lads in their late teens. I quickly realised these locals had tickets to sell, so I jogged my way over. I arrived to hear one English lad say, 'A thousand for two tickets? Fuck off, you thieving bastard.' Most of the other lads also turned away in disgust, and I think if it hadn't been for the police presence these two locals may well have been turned over there and then. I couldn't help but notice the look on these lads' faces as they seemed surprised to be turned down so quickly, so I asked one of them a quick question.

'Is that a thousand francs for two?'

'Yes.'

The pissed-up English prick had turned down the opportunity of a lifetime. The French lad didn't want £1,000, he wanted francs, and that worked out at approximately £100 for the pair, £50 each. A rapid check of the ticket confirmed it wasn't hooky, and the deal was done. To my surprise the lad then pulled a handful of tickets from his back pocket, but before the scrum could begin I was off and into the station. At first I couldn't believe it. This was the game I felt certain I was never going to see, yet now I was the proud owner of a ticket for just fifty bloody quid.

Now, one of my major faults is that I trust people too easily, and as the reality and excitement of getting the ticket began to sink in I very nearly blew it for myself as other supporters

172

came over and I told them about the lad outside. As many of those around me were making their first trip to France '98 I openly passed the ticket around without thinking. I showed them all what to look out for in order to check they weren't getting ripped off when two Stoke City fans suddenly appeared and joined in the conversation. One of these City boys had also bought a ticket from the lad outside, and after a quick check it turned out he was in the seat next to mine, which sparked the following short exchange of words.

'Oh nice one, mate, I'll see you in there.'

To which his mate replied, 'Yeah. Or we could always give you a good kicking and steal your ticket so that we can sit together.'

The words rang in my ears as I rapidly made my way down to the platform and onto a train that was just seconds away from departing. The guard assured me this was the correct train. I then surrounded myself with fellow England fans for safety, only this time keeping my ticket firmly tucked out of sight. I couldn't help wondering whether a fellow England fan would actually beat up one of his own in order to get a ticket. The relief I was now feeling obviously indicated that the threat seemed real enough at the time, so I swore to hate Stoke City and all their fans from that moment on. Thieving gypsy bastards.

The guard at Calais station had given me the correct information, but this train was slow – painfully slow. I had intended to take the train to Lille before making the short trip to Lens, but the police had obviously wanted the England fans out of the station as soon as possible so half of us were shunted onto this milk train and given no choice but to sit the journey out.

While travelling I found myself sitting next to Ian, a Brentford fan, and Chris and Julie, both Gunners. Not one of them had a ticket, but like nearly everyone else on the train felt compelled to make the effort. I couldn't help but think back to that poxy advertising campaign that told people not to travel without tickets. Whoever it was in government that gave the OK to spending God knows how much taxpayers' money on such a pointless exercise should have been sacked immediately as he, or she, obviously has no idea as to what drives the football supporter. I honestly don't think that campaign stopped one person from travelling to France, but what I can say is that personally it made me more determined to prove them wrong. Drink bans stop people, as does failing to show the match in the local bars, but a finger-wagging warning from a government that has proved year after year that it has little love for or understanding of the country's national sport cuts no ice whatsoever. If any government official ever wanted proof of that then he should have been on the 2.15 p.m. train out of Calais station.

Eventually, the Stade Felix-Bollaert, the home of the French league champions Lens, came into sight and that beautiful rush of adrenalin began to flow through my body yet again. The rail track passed within yards of the stadium, with the long road running alongside, providing the first indication as to just how many England fans had made the journey across the Channel in order to cheer their country on to victory.

As the train slowed to a stop I was surprised to see the platform lined with England fans ready to climb on board and head off to Paris. I made my way through the tiny yet bustling station and out onto the main square to be greeted by the heaving sight of thousands of England fans, riot police and camera crews standing around, seemingly not knowing what the hell to do next. The atmosphere was heavy, like no other I had ever experienced at a football match, as the three groups looked on at each other with distrust and disdain. There was no singing from the English, no flag waving and no real camaraderie. The only sound to be heard was a constant rumble of people talking in unhappy tones. The usual laughter and football-related banter were absent to the extreme. Over in the corner was a small but lively group of Colombian fans who seemed intent on ignoring the air of despondency that weighed down on the area, while the local shop and stall holders did their best to look as though they weren't actually shitting themselves as they tried to go about their business.

I have never in my life seen so many people walking around with a hangover in one place. The drink ban had been in place for over nine hours and many of those around were now suffering from the effects of their previous all-night bender. With a distinct lack of tickets, the heavy police presence and nothing to do but sit at the roadside, this made for an uneasy mix. Some England fans were even arguing among themselves, and suddenly an overwhelming desire to hook up with someone I knew came upon me as I seriously began to fear for my own well-being. Groups of police occupied every street corner dressed in full riot gear and ready to go. It was easy to understand their anxiety following the Germany incident, and it was clear to see that many of those in uniform had a look on their faces that expressed a desire to be anywhere else on the planet rather than here. They appeared to have little or no leadership as they just stood and watched, their teargas guns at the ready, but not really knowing what to do.

I soon bumped into a lad I knew from my home town who was just about to do the off and head back out to Lille in the hope of finding a bar in which the game was being shown. He had been in the town the previous night, and he told me that trouble had broken out late on as the police moved in to disperse the large gathering of England fans in the main square. He had been in Lens all day and felt sure things would flare up at any moment as the vibe had been growing steadily worse as the day went on. As far as getting to see the game was concerned, Lens was a definite no-no, with the police intending to shut every bar in the hope that most of the England fans would sod off back across the Channel as soon as possible. He told me that the odd confrontation had already taken place with the police, and then he pointed out a group of lads sitting on a wall who were intending to steam into the Colombian fans as soon as they found themselves unprotected by the police whom they had carefully latched themselves onto. The reason for this was that the Central Americans had tickets for sale by the bus load and had been busy touting them around all day long. Unfortunately for my mate, they were asking £400 a shot. But the word was spreading that in due course they would be relieved of them for slightly less.

By this time many England fans had given up the ghost and decided to look elsewhere for a place to watch the match. Some had more luck than others, and once again Sharon and her mates from Kent turned up a nice little tickle:

When we arrived in Lens it was like walking into the middle of London, English everywhere. We knew there was hardly any chance of getting tickets, but we had an added problem as we had all our bags with us as we were going on to a camp site in Bordeaux for a week afterwards. There was nowhere for us to leave everything, so we gave up looking pretty early as we wanted to make sure we could at least get to see the game on telly.

While we were trying to make up our minds what to do next we got talking to this Scottish guy called Willie, who turned out to be a godsend. What he was doing here with all these English was hard to work out at first, but he must have felt a bit outnumbered. He was a really nice bloke and offered to give us a lift to the hotel we had booked for the night. On the journey we found out he was actually an overseas scout for West Ham United and he really knew his football. He obviously knew we wanted to see the game, so he offered to wait for us while we checked in and then take us to a bar he knew where the game was being shown. We ended up in a small village in the middle of nowhere, but as we went to enter the bar the owner suddenly refused us entry due to the drink ban. Willie then got on his mobile phone and rang a mate of his who was apparently a friend of the Mayor of Lens. We stood around not knowing what the hell was going on, but one call led to another before the owner came out smiling and let us in. He had just been given permission by the mayor to serve us beer as we were with

Willie, but only us four and no one else, which, considering we were in the arse end of nowhere, seemed unlikely anyway.

Once inside we joined the locals and got pissed as farts while watching England. The locals were so friendly towards us, and when we won they brought us drink after drink to celebrate. We had a fantastic night, unforgettable really. It could only have been bettered by actually being there in the flesh.

Despite the ban on alcohol there were still plenty of beer bottles on show, and while some of the police let that pass unchecked, others were proving a little less tolerant. As I stood surveying the scene a group of around ten policemen was making its way towards the square from the direction of the stadium. Suddenly one of the officers broke ranks and walked over to a lad who was sitting at the kerbside drinking a bottle of lager. Without warning the policeman knocked the bottle from his hand with his truncheon and sent it spinning away on the tarmac. Whether this officer had had a bad day or not I don't know, but his actions were totally unnecessary, threatening and provocative.

The lad reacted in the same way as 90 per cent of the population would under such circumstances: he jumped to his feet and shouted at the officer. The policeman, already well-balanced with a chip on each shoulder, and obviously on edge, saw himself under threat and his colleagues ran to his call. Together they pushed the lad back against the fence and surrounded him while they formed a wall facing out towards the onlooking crowd. The victim's mates began to shout at the police, and more cries from angry Englishmen began to fill the air. A bottle was then thrown in the direction of the coppers and shouts of 'Do the Old Bill' began to ring out loudly. Suddenly a mass of bodies came running up the hill from the direction of the stadium – not more police or supporters, but film crews, probably ten in all. As the lad struggled for freedom the cameras rolled and the sound man got the cries he needed for the news footage that would soon be sent across the globe. These were then backed up by the pictures of the lad in question being led away handcuffed and face down by riot police with truncheons drawn.

Why that lad was picked out for such treatment I'll never know. There were literally hundreds of Englishmen doing exactly the same as him, just drinking by the side of the road. If the police had wanted him to stop then why didn't they just tell him to pour the lot away rather than use such violent actions? Was it some kind of shock tactic, or was the policeman just a power-crazed arsehole? Whatever it was, the action taken very nearly sparked off an incident that would once more have had the name of English football dragged through the gutter. What happened to that lad then was disgusting; what happened after they had taken him away doesn't bear thinking about. And the consequences for his personal life could prove disastrous if he were to end up in court, convicted and either put in prison or deported. Back home the press would have another front-page picture and no politician in his right mind would come to the defence of such a hooligan. Proof once again that if you happen to be an English football supporter abroad your life can go tits up in the time it takes to wet your whistle.

While the north of France resembled a country under siege, way down south in Bordeaux my friend Pete was having a whale of a time:

If Monday night's game with Romania had been an English love-in, then this could only be described as a full-on, no-holds-barred gang bang. English fans had poured into the city from all over as news had spread that Bordeaux was the place to be if you didn't have a ticket for the game. Even the worry of being in the same city as the Argentines and their Nazi head cases didn't put the English off as they came in hope, in good spirits and in the mood to party.

While the Argies and the Croats fought it out up the

road we played our football matches by the big screen: North v. South, Premier League v. Nationwide, or Moan Utd v. anyone else. Every club in the country was represented in Bordeaux, and it was fucking marvellous to be part of it. During the week I sat on the beach with Croatians, big scary blokes eager to show me their bullet wounds, drank with Scots, Americans and South Africans, and shook hands with Argies, but now I was well and truly among my own lovely, lovely English men, women and children.

I met a young lady called Claire whom I had to pretend was my sister following some rather unsavoury advances from a couple of West Ham fans. We got on so well that later that night the pair of us could have been arrested for incest, although I must admit that that little game added a strange tinge to the moment.

Outnumbered and downtrodden following their defeat against Morocco, the Scots kept their distance as we rejoiced at Anderton's shot, Beckham's free kick and a display that filled the heart with joy. Rumour had it that people were paying £500 plus for a ticket in Lens; we had all this for nothing. I wanted to be part of this World Cup. I wanted to say I was there at France '98 and now I can hold my head up high. I wouldn't have missed this experience for the world, and I didn't have to haggle with some tout, suck up to the Football Association, or pay out a month's wages for the pleasure!

Back up in Lens the atmosphere grew more depressed by the second. I really began to fear that I could soon find myself trapped in a similar situation as the lad just drinking in the street, a situation from which there was no escape. Being the proud owner of a ticket I decided that my best course of action was to get myself away from this square and down towards the stadium, so I began the walk down the main drag. Pretty soon my path was blocked as the police had thrown a human barrier across the road through which only those with match tickets were allowed to pass. I happily held out my ticket for all to see when suddenly the unthinkable happened as it was taken from my palm and subjected to serious scrutiny by a very large, tooled-up policeman.

As he stared back my stomach sank. This was the first time someone had actually lived out the warnings and checked up on a ticket. I was so sure it wouldn't happen that I hadn't even looked at the name printed upon it myself, but I was pretty sure it wasn't Mr J. Smith. I could feel the sweat rolling down my head as I nervously smiled back, then after what seemed like an eternity he handed back the ticket and begrudgingly moved aside. I checked the name printed: M. Courvoisier. Me? I don't think so somehow, but I wasn't going back to argue the fact.

Behind the police cordon there was more of the same: England fans looking bored, aimless and on edge. There were more camera crews and news reporters here than on the other side, and riot police by the bus load just standing around, kitted out with guns in hand, ready for action. Not one person appeared to have a clue as to what they should do. The actual entrances to the stadium were still locked, so with well over three hours to kick-off the English and Colombians were just killing time by sitting on the grass bank. Most had fixed themselves a view back up the main drag that provided a perfect vantage point just in case anything were to flare up, but for the most part they were just twiddling their thumbs. The majority of the police looked like they were shitting themselves, every sound sending heads turning, followed by long, hard stares. Some of the police had also secured good vantage points and were standing in silence among the English. All this for a football match. Total madness. And to think that within two weeks of the new season starting back home they'll be telling us football hasn't got a hooligan problem any more.

I honestly felt the drink ban that had been imposed was a good idea. I totally understood the reasons why the police were so on edge, but I couldn't for the life of me find a reason for shutting down the big screen that was due to show the match later that night. Someone had fucked up big time if they thought the supporters would just get bored and leave. For one, there wasn't enough transport to allow anyone to get anywhere anyway – few trains and not one bus; and two, as long as there was an outside chance of a ticket, most would rather sit it out, hoping for that stroke of luck that would see them inside the stadium come nine o'clock. If only they had provided some kind of distraction then everyone's minds would have had something else to focus on, rather than staring at line after line of riot police. As I joined the throng gazing back up the hill towards the train station at least I was safe in the knowledge that I had a reason for being here and something to look forward to.

Desperately, I searched among the passing masses for a face I recognised, then out of the blue my eyes fell upon a lanky, lurching piece of string that could only be Tony. To my delight, walking alongside was Gary whose ticket had obviously survived the wrath of his wife's scissors. Herne Bay was also there, so at last I began to feel safe and less of an easy target. All of us agreed that we had never experienced an atmosphere such as this before, and not one of us could understand why those in charge insisted on locking us outside the stadium, as letting us in would at least remove half of the problem for the police.

The three of them had spent the previous night in Lille where they had witnessed some of the trouble that had been reported. Thankfully they had managed to stay out of the way and ended up doing an all-night session and getting totally slaughtered. Gary soon told me that Mr B was also with them at first, but ended up getting so pissed that he was in no fit state to travel anywhere. He had remained in Lille in the hope of finding a bar in which to watch the game, along with a few thousand others.

Eventually we decided to move away from the roundabout and head off to wait by the gates of the stadium. As we wandered down the road we found ourselves walking at the back of yet another group of corporate ticket holders and prize winners wearing Snickers badges. Suddenly, a lad sitting on the grass bank started shouting in our direction. We soon realised his verbal was being directed straight at us as he had made the mistake of believing we were part of the chocolate bar gang. Under the circumstances this was a major slur, and Herne Bay quickly took offence at this lad's suggestions to go forth and multiply. The noise level soon began to rise as Herne Bay firmly put the lad in place by listing every England away game he had attended for the last ten years, adding that he had never seen that lad's face on any of those trips. This was all we needed, a fight among ourselves. As the police began to turn their eyes on the situation, the mouthy one thankfully bottled out and Herne Bay eventually let it lie.

For the next 40 minutes we walked aimlessly around the stadium until the gates finally opened. Unlike Toulouse, those in charge at Lens had showed little, if any, imagination as far as pre-match entertainment was concerned, unless of course you had a pass that allowed you inside one of the many hospitality tents that flanked the car park. Once again I found myself with a ticket situated at the far end of the stadium from where the bulk of the English support was to be positioned, so with little over an hour to kick-off I said goodbye to the others and headed off towards my entrance.

I found following England to be much the same as any other form of travelling, in as much as the same old faces seem to pop up wherever you go. Once again I bumped into the lads from Exeter I had met on my very first night in Marseille, only this time they were looking a little less excited. They told me that after this match they were off home and couldn't wait to get back to Blighty. They had heard a rumour that some lads from their local rivals Plymouth were on the look-out for them, and as they were now down to around six in total it was something they didn't really need. I had heard stories of Portsmouth and Southampton fans fighting in Toulouse, but this was the only other incident I had been told about where English lads were prepared to carry their local battles across the water. Usually all that stuff is left behind at the ferry terminal or airport as the mentality of 'all English together' takes over. Just being English posed enough problems. If it were true, then it was out of order that these lads were given yet more hassle to worry about.

As we talked I was able to check out the main entrance to my part of the stadium. The inspection my ticket had received at the road block had made me a little less confident of walking straight up to the gate, and the sight of yet another ten ticket checkers backed up by a line of riot police didn't ease the worries that much. As I looked on another lad joined me, obviously playing the same game. I soon found out that he had an added worry as his ticket was even hotter than mine. Like many others he had been approached by the Colombians up at the station and offered tickets at £300. Obviously he had refused, but along with a couple of mates had cleverly sat back and studied the movements of the men selling the tickets. They had watched and followed their every move for over two hours before finally sending one of their group forward, making out he wanted to make a purchase. The others had already moved off into the area where the deal was to be done, and when the tout and their friend arrived they quickly set about relieving the tout of the tickets he had hoped to sell. Now let me state here and now that mugging isn't something I usually support, but on this occasion you have to ask yourself who was trying to mug whom? Personally, I think fair play to the lad, but I declined his offer of swapping tickets as I didn't want to be the one sitting next to an irate Central American ticket tout with a bump on his head.

As kick-off got nearer the crowds grew thick, so the time had come to bundle my way in and hope that the sheer weight of numbers would help me to force my way through without any problems. As ever in situations like these, the butterflies rose as every step took me nearer, then the moment came as the ticket was taken from my hand and given the once over. Desperately I tried to look as French as possible, that smug shaking of the head, one eye slightly closed, the lip curl. What I would have given for a blue and white hooped shirt, a string of garlic and a crap old bicycle at that moment. The bloke with the ticket then threw a look over his shoulder at one of the policemen behind, and for a split second I really thought I wasn't going to make it. Fortunately for me the checker's look wasn't returned and the mumbling of those pushing behind me forced his hand. Unwillingly he gave me back the ticket along with a knowing look, and through I went.

Not wishing to push my luck any further I decided there and then to find my seat and stay firmly in position until kick-off. The climb up the concrete stairway was long, but the sight that greeted me was well worth the effort. The Stade Felix-Bollaert is a magnificent stadium, one of the best I have ever been fortunate enough to visit. The stands are steep and tall giving an unbelievable view of the pitch, and the angled roof traps the noise providing a superb atmosphere. The local supporters fill this ground to the rafters week in, week out, and it is easy to see why.

Unlike many European grounds, this was nothing but a football arena. It had character. It forced you to watch the action taking place on the lush green turf. This cauldron almost begged you to join in the singing. It twisted your arm to be part of the event. As we continue to build those so-called state-of-the-art stadiums back home, with that ever-so-nineties feel – lack of character, toilet space and leg room – we kill off stadiums such as these. Why?

The volume being generated by the English fans at the far end of the ground was like nothing else I had encountered. The passion in that noise must surely be worth a goal start to any side, and considering the importance of the result the optimism of my fellow countrymen could only result in there being one final outcome: an England victory. All the doubts I had had before kick-off about the final result were beaten into submission as I watched the dancing, took in the singing and listened to the band as they fired up yet another song. I would have given anything to be in that end of the stadium, but once more I was surrounded by Frenchmen and supporters from every other country that happened to be taking part in this tournament. I'll give them some credit – they were enjoying if for all it was worth – but I couldn't help but become a little angry as I asked myself yet again the question, why were they here? This wasn't about them or their country, this was about the spirit of being English. Sod the unity of the World Cup. This was our day, we had to get a result here and our country needed us, not them. I prayed for support myself, but the lad from Stoke who had bought the seat next to mine never made it, so my nearest soulmate in an England shirt was over ten seats away, but still giving it his best shot none the less.

I wondered what the feeling was back home. Were the pubs and clubs of England sharing the same optimism as was being generated within this stadium? I believe that passion is what the majority want to see when their team takes to the field in order to represent the people. At times like this every one of us belongs to the masses, sharing a common bond and a love for our country. Were the Scots looking on, already knocked out, praying for a Colombian win? Of course they were, but for the next 90 minutes they – and the rest of the world – were going to have 'Ing-ger-land!' rammed right down their throats as the fans, the players and the country celebrated what we hoped would prove to be a famous victory. The atmosphere quickly whipped up those same old feelings inside.

I love it. I love being English. As the old song goes, 'No one likes us, we don't care', and at this moment I couldn't give a fuck what anyone else thinks of us. In fact, I don't want anyone to like us, because then, when we win, even more people get that losing feeling. I love winning. It doesn't happen that often, but when it does I love it. I want to rub everyone else's nose in it. There are some people who hate talk like that, the do-gooders and the politically correct. The very people who wouldn't be seen dead in football land are the ones who tell us we're wrong. Wankers. I hate political correctness. Why do we have to listen to people who continually tell us we're wrong to feel this way? What's so bad about wanting to come out on top? Competition is good, it drives people forward. The world doesn't switch on to see an even-handed contest, they want someone, or some team, to get stuffed. When you follow England you know that 99.9 per cent of the watching world want your team to get stuffed, so when you end up winning it makes it even better. The Scottish understand that; they love to display their passion. They love to give it loads. The Chilean players understand that too; you could see it when they sung their national anthem. I love to see that. It's real, passionate, alive.

First Anderton, then Beckham. England 2, Colombia 0. 'No one likes us, we don't care' – never a truer word spoken. If this wasn't a football night to remember then I've never had one. When the final whistle blew a warm glow rippled through my body. It was a winning glow, a glow that told me most of Scotland was unhappy, that most of the world was unhappy. Yet all I could hear were the joyous cries of my fellow countrymen ringing loudly in my ears. Oh deep, deep joy.

The mood displayed by the England fans on the road back up to the train station couldn't have been more of a contrast to the one this same street had witnessed prior to kick-off. The small roundabout at the bottom of the hill had been taken over by celebrating fans as they danced and sang for the gathering camera crews. The riot police looked on, massed together and still on edge. They need not have worried; England had got the result and in a way that meant that they had as well. Surprisingly, Romania only managed a 1–1 draw with the Tunisians, but it was enough to secure them top spot in the group.

While we celebrated the victory in France, back home in England the mood fuelled by the mixture of pubs, football and Friday-night drinking soon boiled over into violence come chucking-out time. In one small Hertfordshire town an estimated crowd of 125 flooded the streets and entered into confrontation with the police. Bottles and cans were thrown and passing cars were kicked; seven people appeared in court the following Monday morning. Such incidents were repeated throughout the country as police authorities found themselves stretched to the limit. God only knows what would have happened had England lost.

All I wanted to do was get back home. As expected, the station was rammed with fans being sent in all directions – the usual French form of organised chaos. In reality it was just chaos, as those in control had failed to arrange special trains in order to get us away and up to the ferry terminals at Calais and Boulogne in time to make connecting ferries. With the next train north not due for another hour, I sat myself down and was suddenly overtaken by exhaustion as the day's events finally caught up. The added realisation that I would now miss my ferry strengthened the tiredness, as England now seemed a few hours further away.

I began the long wait alone, feeling like a 'Billy no mates', and contemplated England's next match. The results from today's other games had gone pretty much to plan, with Argentina beating Croatia 1–0 and Jamaica winning 2–1 against Japan. These results meant that England now had the unenviable task of playing the Argies, a team that had won all three of their group games, scored seven goals in the process and conceded none!

England v. Argentina. Now that will be some battle, almost as big as the one I am going to be faced with when I tell the wife, 'I'll just be popping out for a few hours again then, dear!'

Tired
Day 18: Saturday, 27 June

Eventually the train turns up and the slow journey north begins. On arriving at Calais the French finally come up trumps and appear to have something organised, with buses laid on to move us quickly across town. The flashing blue lights of the police vans help our vehicles snake their way through the deserted streets as though we're involved in some kind of military manoeuvre to rid France of undesirables, which is actually closer to the truth than I'd like to think.

Once inside the terminal building I am again surrounded by the familiar disorganisation I've come to expect of France '98. With the next Sea France crossing not due to leave for another two and a half hours, I decide to take a walk around to the departure doors where people are queuing to board a P&O Stena ferry shipping out in less than 30 minutes. I quickly come across a guy who has just helped himself to a handful of duty free shopping vouchers which he believes are also usable as boarding passes. He gives me a spare and I decide to try my luck and join the long line of paying punters as they file their way past the check point. Amazingly, I walk through without so much as a bonjour from the tired staff. I jump on the buses and some ten minutes later there I am sitting in the coffee lounge waiting to be served.

The slow motion of the ferry soon tells me we are on our

way, and I can't help but feel a little pleased with myself, as bunking a ferry is most certainly a new one in the Brimson household. I like the idea of being a stowaway, but it's more likely that the French authorities just wanted as many English as possible out of the way quickly, and couldn't really be arsed to check the ticket.

One and a half hours later I am in my car heading back home wondering whether or not I am going to fall asleep at the wheel and kill myself. Somehow I survive the M25 and at six o'clock I climb into bed, totally cream-crackered.

Every football fan I have ever talked to has days that will live in the memory for ever. These are the days that make up for all the shit we have to put up with. Some of those days are remembered for the events on the football field, some for everything else that comes with being a footy fan. The last 22 hours have provided me with one of those special days. This trip had everything a supporter of the greatest game in the world could ever want. These are the days that keep us going back for more, the matches that will have us telling the story for years to come. England v. Colombia, I was there. I wouldn't have missed this for the world and I had managed to do it all for under £100. What an unbelievable result that was. Oh, I love the god that is football.

My much-needed sleep is disrupted by the searing sound of my alarm clock. This was the day the World Cup should really have started in earnest, as we had now reached the proper knockout stages of the tournament, meaning no second chances for any side. At 3.00 p.m. I sit myself down in front of the telly, matchsticks at the ready if needed to keep my eyes open, and watch the Italians take on Norway. Considering what is at stake, this is a piss-poor excuse for a game, and with hindsight I really should have stayed in my pit. Italy win 1–0 thanks to a goal from Vieri in the eighteenth minute. On hitting the back of the net, Mr Vieri and a few chums in their celebration run to the touchline and sit down cross-legged, looking like a group of naughty school children. In fact they look like a bunch of wankers, as does any player taking part in such tomfoolery. To think they actually spend time talking such things through! Whatever happened to that manly jog back to the centre circle, let's-get-on-with-the-game attitude? The Italian victory, despite such a poor performance, has me thinking uneasily that they could well be the team with their name on the cup.

The other game played out today is the all-South American affair between Brazil and Chile, a match I desperately want Salas and co. to win. Unfortunately, my prayers go unanswered, the game all but sealed for Brazil by half-time. The final outcome is a 4–1 victory for the pre-tournament favourites. At the time the match appears to take a back seat in the mind of the producer as we are suddenly treated to more pictures of Ronaldo's girlfriend than the actual match. We also get the beautiful vision of Michel Platini taking part in the Mexican wave. Poor man – as if he hasn't got enough to be embarrassed about already, what with the ticket sham and all that.

The Boring Art of Making History
Day 19: Sunday, 28 June

Today I find myself desperately ringing around friends and lonely hearts columns in order to get a travelling companion for my next trip out. While on the trip to Lens I had started to notice people looking at me in a that-bloke's-got-no-mates kind of way, something that had got so bad I now have to prove to myself they were wrong. It is a difficult job, but the constant tugging at the heart strings and arm-twisting finally pay off when my friend Smurf agrees to 'Eddy sit'. See, I do have friends – well, one anyway.

In terms of World Cup football this is an historic day. For the first time a 'golden goal' settles a finals match. The lucky winners of this particular page in the history books are the host nation, Laurent Blanc scoring the winner for France in the twenty-fourth minute of extra time against Paraguay, following a 0–0 bore draw. France really are poor, crap in fact, as they ride their luck on more than one occasion. It's luck that again has me thinking the worst. But no, surely the slug eaters won't win it!

With the competition at the knockout stage, the Danes remind us that all previous results count for nothing by turning the form book upside down and hammering Nigeria 4–1. The result fills me with both sadness at seeing the Africans sent packing, and optimism, because if this Danish side can win, anyone can on their day.

A day of bad news ends on the lowest note of all as reports come through claiming that Sir Alf Ramsey is in hospital suffering from a mild heart attack.

Just Popping Out Again, Love
Day 20: Monday, 29 June

As expected, I spent most of the day trying to make conversation with a woman who was going to bleed the situation for all it was worth. The wife was making me suffer for yet another trip. Her indoors relentlessly pointed out the lack of new clothes in her wardrobe, the odd jobs around the flat and the fact that she hadn't had a holiday so far this year. Holiday! What did she think I was doing, going out on the piss? Spending time with the lads? Indulging in my favourite hobby while she sat at home? For Christ's sake, love, I am trying to earn a living. It's a dirty job, I know, but someone's got to do it. Admittedly I was on dodgy ground, but I stuck to the argument that I was just working. I tried to convince her that I was carrying out research, trying to build a better future and all that crap, but the look in her eye told me that by now my defence had worn thinner than my hairline.

The arrival of my fellow traveller, Smurf, rescued me from the torture. In an instant this old hag before me turned into the loving, caring female that makes me the envy of all my friends. A kiss on the cheek, the offer of a lovingly put together packed lunch and the blessing of the Virgin Mary to protect us on our expedition. All switched on like the illuminations at Blackpool. Not wishing to push my luck, I decided to give the first half of Germany v. Mexico a miss and quit while I was ahead. The final cuddle at the doorstep was tinged a little as she 'accidentally' managed to tread on my toes while squeezing me a little too hard for comfort, but fuck it, I was released and off once again.

Within an hour Smurf and I were sitting in a bar just around the corner from Victoria station, downing a few jars while awaiting the arrival of the coach. For a Monday afternoon the pub was pretty full, with one group in particular making more noise than anyone else. The centre of attention for this mainly female group was what can only be described as a pig of a bloke wearing an England shirt. For some reason the young ladies in the group were all over this lad, so much so that if he'd had a shitty stick it would surely have been called into use in order to beat the buggers away. When he came to the bar we began talking, and I soon found out that he was about to leave for Turkey on holiday and all the girls from the office had come to see him off. After a while we could resist it no longer and had to ask what it was he had that made him so popular with the ladies. His answer was thus:

First off, I am the office gay, which means all the girls want to mother me. Secondly, they all want to be the one to 'change me'. Which they can't, but they see it as the ultimate challenge. And thirdly, I am hung like a donkey, which adds to them wanting to change me. It also has them thinking that even if I don't enjoy it, they will!

My mother always told me never to speak to strangers, and for the first time I fully understood what she meant. Once again I was scared. Thank God Smurf was with me, as there is not much you can say to an answer like that.

Very, very quickly we finished our drinks and headed for the coach pick-up point. By six o'clock we were safely on board and heading out of the capital towards Folkestone and the Channel Tunnel. To my surprise, the coach was less than half full, the majority being Aston Villa fans. Only a few had vouchers to exchange for match tickets, the rest, like us, just chancers who couldn't resist the pull of such an important game. Thankfully, the lack of numbers allowed every one of us two seats in which to stretch out.

With the coach slowly heading south, I was reminded why I had avoided this form of transport so far. Getting some shut eye wasn't going to be easy, especially when the news that the sausage eaters had beaten Mexico with two late goals had us all fearing that the trophy had Germany's name on it.

Serious Argy-Bargy
Day 21: Tuesday, 30 June

Finding a position comfortable enough in which to sleep proved impossible, until approximately 6.30 in the morning. At 6.45 I was woken by my so-called friend so that I wouldn't miss breakfast at the motorway service station, and, once lost, that one and only sleeping position was never to be found again. What a bastard.

At ten o'clock we found ourselves to be the first supporters coach to arrive in St Etienne and, surprise surprise, no one was there to greet us. We drove around and around the stadium for about half an hour before a man appeared and directed us away from the ground and off into the outback. We eventually arrived at a park full of five-a-side pitches and tennis courts where we were told to park up, disembark, and then catch a courtesy bus back to the stadium. Over on one of the pitches the occupants of a small group of tents and camper vans housing England fans were now indulging in an early-morning kickabout. The lads who had travelled down with vouchers were beginning to panic as they had to exchange them for match tickets before one o'clock, and time was quickly running out. As Smurf and I had to fend for ourselves we left them to it and headed off to catch a bus into the main part of the town.

We were joined by Keith, a bloke in his early fifties who had also made the coach journey with us. Unfortunately for him he was the only Birmingham City fan on the bus among all those Villa fans, so he had until now kept himself to himself. He told us that this was the first trip he had made so far to France '98. Before the competition started he had sworn to himself that if England were to play the Argies then he would do all he could to see it live. Two more lads who had been camping in the field soon came to join the queue, and told us that ticket prices had dropped to £100 the previous night, news that had us all forgetting the crap night we had just had to endure as our chances of getting a ticket appeared to increase tenfold. A hundred pounds was well within all our price ranges.

As the bus took us in towards the main square our hopes were higher than they had ever been. The two lads also issued us a warning, telling us to watch our backs, that the night before groups of locals were driving around and picking off England fans who were walking around on their own or in small groups. To back up their story they went on to tell us of one lad camping near them who had been well and truly beaten up before having everything on him stolen. They also went on to say that the night before had gone off well until eleven o'clock, then suddenly the police became heavy-handed and started shutting the bars without warning. They then lined up in full riot gear and started banging away on their shields as if baiting the England fans, the reaction being a short flurry of bottle throwing. The coppers then steamed in, scattering most but arresting a few.

Following the ten-minute bus ride we arrived in the main square. The scare stories put around by the press back home had obviously been taken at face value by many as it became obvious that fewer England fans had been prepared to chance it on this trip than for any of the other matches. For us three that was good news as it meant less competition for tickets, which in turn should have meant a lower asking price. The good behaviour shown by the English fans in both Toulouse and Lens had finally led to a relaxing of the drinking ban and the switching on of the big screen that had taken up position in the main square. It almost felt like parents finding out that they had blamed the wrong child, so now we were allowed to watch the TV again.

That aside, I have to say that in my opinion whoever it was that gave the thumbs up to providing such entertainment deserved a medal. At last the message had got home that a little trust can go a long way, as bands performed for the supporters soaking up the sun. The relaxed atmosphere had the English and Argentinians mixing happily while the police enjoyed an easier afternoon than they could ever have hoped for. I swear you could see the disbelief and disappointment on the faces of many camera crews and journalists as they watched the two sets of fans mixing together. The media did have their hopes lifted briefly as a group of Stockport County fans took the bandstand and began belting out 'You'll never take the Falklands', but as the cameras started rolling the rest of us laughed more at them than anything else.

Admittedly, I hadn't expected to see such a friendly atmosphere myself. The Falklands conflict is only recent history, and the potential for trouble was always a major worry in the build-up to this day. Thankfully it just didn't happen, and I believe that one of the main reasons for this was the fact that we all found ourselves in the same boat as far as our first priority was concerned, which was of course getting tickets for the game. Following on from all the hype it was a joy to see and a pleasure to be part of such a relaxed atmosphere, but the three of us couldn't help thinking what the press were making of it back home! Almost certainly there were more English on the hunt than Argies, but both sets of fans were united in their desire to get to see the match and their frustration with the blatant ticket-touting that was taking place wherever you looked.

Any hopes we had of finding cheap tickets were soon dashed as we quickly found the asking price to be stuck at the £300 mark. Many of the English had decided yet again that the best option was just to sit tight, enjoy a few sherbets and wait until the last possible moment in the hope that prices would fall. Whereas they had taken the decision to chill out rather than waste their time haggling with the locals, I just couldn't let the time slip by without at least trying. The next few hours were spent walking from street to street asking every Frenchman and his poodle whether or not they had a ticket for sale, and as time wore on the thrill of being at the world's greatest sporting event was increasingly beginning to lose its shine. Once again it seemed that every local chancer had taken the opportunity to buy his or her one ticket before hiking up the price and selling it on. Men, women and even children, well dressed and ready to rip off the thousands of desperate football fans for as much as possible. Alongside them were the organised groups of youths, carefully being directed by people waiting up in the shadows of the back streets.

Wherever someone stopped in the hope of doing a deal, groups of youths crowded around making the transaction as difficult as possible for those involved. Increasingly, many of the English were beginning to air the opinion that they were mighty fucked off as the price remained ridiculously high, and in the middle of the square I watched as two lads began talking money with a local youth who had been doing the rounds all afternoon. Immediately a crowd grew in the hope of hearing that the price was at last about to start falling. On hearing the asking price of £300 I once again began to walk away in disgust, and was surprised that the English lad was willing to pay, when suddenly things began to hot up. On counting the money the local tout realised that only £200 had been handed over and he began demanding the additional hundred. The England fan just turned away, ignoring the request and laughing with his pal, but before the congratulations of his fellow Englishman could subside local youths had appeared from all directions and were beginning to crowd around. The English lad soon found himself well and truly outnumbered. Vainly he searched out support from those around him, but the throat-cutting gestures being directed his way soon had the rest of us turning our gaze towards the local architecture. Thankfully the lad stood tall while slowly but surely manoeuvring his body in the direction of the nearest policeman, but I still can't help feeling a little ashamed at my willingness to turn away, along with another six or seven Englishmen.

When you find yourself in situations such as these you quickly become an expert in the art of clutching at straws, so when Keith reappeared with a rumour about tickets selling cheaper up at the stadium we very quickly jumped on the first bus heading that way. It didn't take us long to find that we had headed off chasing nothing more than a red herring, but just as disturbing a find was the sight of police check points that had been set up to keep the ticketless fans well away from the stadium area. That sight gave me a real sinking feeling, and for the first time I felt as if this was going to be one game I would fail to see.

Up until that moment Smurf, Keith and myself had worked together in the hope of finding a ticket, but here we made the decision that from now on it was every man for himself. Unanimously we voted to head back to the centre, not only to look for a ticket but also to search out the nearest bar in which to watch the game when all else failed. We returned to the main square only to find the same faces trying to sell the same tickets at the same price to the same people.

Suddenly I began to question why I was even here. I began to feel genuinely angry. I was hundreds of miles from home busting my nuts while greedy French bastards openly went about the business of ripping me off. There was absolutely nothing I could do but plead with people who appeared to enjoy the fact that they had me by the bollocks, and now I was no longer willing to play the game. For the hundredth time I bumped into two student girls who had been offering their tickets to me all day long, but only at the price of £250 each. When they told me they needed that much money so that they could go on holiday it rammed the message a little too far down my throat for my liking. Holiday! Bitches!

Then came the news that tipped me over the edge: despite the good behaviour of the fans, the big screen that had just finished showing Croatia's 1–0 win over Romania was to be turned off. The police were also refusing to allow local bar owners the opportunity to cash in while showing the match, so once again the England fans were to be left with nothing to do but get well and truly pissed off. For me that was it.

Fuck the lot of it. Fuck the World Cup. Fuck these thieving French bastards. Fuck the FA for shafting our ticket allocation. Fuck football and fuck the England team.

All the anger I have ever felt towards those who have stolen the game from the fans came to a head there and then. At that moment I would have given anything to be transported back home so that I could be in the local with my mates rather than in this piss-poor hovel known as France. Thousands of us had spent hundreds of pounds, taken weeks off work and put up with shite by the bucketload following England, only to be shafted even harder when the big pay-off game came along.

For Smurf this was his first taste of disappointment, so I told him that if a ticket came along he could have it. I had already seen England play and I swore I wasn't going to give any other fucker the privilege of dipping his hand in my pocket so that he could squeeze my nuts. Suddenly, a local appeared and offered Smurf a ticket at what we thought was £100. Very quickly they did the deal before too many could crowd around, then as quick as it had happened the Froggy started ranting that he had been short-changed. His shouting soon attracted the attention of those around us as Smurf struggled to understand this lad's anger. Quickly a fellow Frenchman explained that the asking price was £300, not the £100 Smurf had handed over. I could tell that Smurf didn't fancy the thought of being pursued by a gang of locals, as we had seen happen earlier in the day, so I for one didn't blame him for giving the ticket back without hesitation and admitting a genuine mistake. Other Englishmen were not so forgiving, finding it hard to believe that he actually had a match ticket in his paws and then given it back. The phrase 'some kind of wanker' suddenly became the most common form of abuse heading his way for the next few minutes.

With little over an hour to go before kick-off Smurf and Keith decided that they would like one last stab up at the ground. With little else for me to do I tagged along, dragging my heels as we went. As far as I was concerned I was out of the race. All I wanted to do was get back on the coach and get home, and I wasn't alone in my anger or disappointment. A busload of unhappy England fans is something you wouldn't wish on anybody, and if an official from the Football Association had been on board he would have been hung, drawn and quartered before he could have muttered the words 'I'm all right, Jack'.

On the bus with us was a small family on their way to meet up with a friend who was looking after their match tickets. The father of the group quickly took pity on us and informed us that the friend they were meeting with, although English, actually lived in St Etienne and owned a car sales garage up by the stadium. They had spoken to him earlier in the day and he had hinted to them that he might have a spare to sell if they came across a friend, so once the bus stopped we stuck to them like glue. As we stepped off the bus the garage appeared in front of us, but after a few moments the father returned with the bad news that the spare had just been sold.

This time we arrived near the stadium to find the place crammed and yet another police cordon thrown across the road. This barrier made it virtually impossible to get within half a mile of the ground, so it appeared the dream was over, even for Smurf and Keith. To my disbelief, moving about among the thousands of disappointed Englishmen were locals still openly cashing in on their tickets. With the minutes flying by I couldn't help but think they were beginning to play a very risky game. These were many of the same touts that had been ripping people off and rubbing our noses in it all day long in the main square, and at this stage, with nothing to lose, some England fans were starting to think about settling the score. Following on from the day I'd had, I am sorry to say that I would have found the temptation hard to resist if things did get a little heated, so I stood by and watched the situation unfold before me. The tense atmosphere was heightened as Keith became the centre of attention in an argument that had sparked up around him. The bluenose had picked on one of the touts, launching a torrent of abuse, but the local was standing firm and giving as good back. This, I thought, was it. All eyes turned their way, but once again the England fans seemed reluctant to go for it, leaving Keith to fend for himself before slowly backing down.

The sight of four Mexican fans heading my way soon had the frustration rising inside me once again. Their request – 'We need four tickets' – was met with the short, heartfelt reply it deserved. They needed tickets my arse. Here was the perfect example of just how bad a job the French had made of organising this tournament. What the hell were four Mexicans doing here asking for tickets among all these Englishmen? For ten minutes I stood helplessly by, watching Norwegians, South Africans, Brazilians and supporters from most of the other countries file their way through the line of police, tickets in hand and head towards the stadium. Yet all us England fans could do was gaze in envy as the sight tore our guts out.

Eventually I began to pace up and down, grumbling away to myself, and somehow I then found myself embroiled in an argument with two lads from Oxford. One was sitting down, pissed and mouthy, the other standing and quickly on the defensive following a swift barrage of vicious verbal. For some reason the mouthy twat on the floor got it into his head that I was an undercover English copper checking the crowd for known faces. You what? As if I wasn't pissed off enough already, without this prick getting on my case. Over the years I have had many insults directed my way, and for the most part it has now become mere water off a duck's back, but being branded a copper is something I find hard to cope with. There are various reasons for this that I need not go into within the pages of this book, but this accusation had me well and truly rattled. Here I was in a poxy French hole, without a ticket, half an hour before the kick-off of the biggest game of football I could ever have been hopeful of seeing, and I find myself arguing with some carrot-crunching wank breath. After about two minutes of well-based, eloquently put reasoning, I think I managed to convince them of my leanings as the pair soon fucked off leaving me to get on with the job in hand – that of feeling well miffed.

As I turned, huffing and puffing, to gaze once more at the police line, I suddenly found myself nose to nose with a garlic muncher who was about to turn my world upside down.

'You need a ticket?'

At first he whispered the words from the corner of his mouth so as not to alert anyone else to the nature of his business. A French Arthur Daley if ever there was one.

'How much?'

'Three thousand francs.'

Now by this time I had become accustomed to telling the thieving bastards to head off in search of horizontal refreshment, but for some reason I asked him to hand over the ticket so that I could check it out. While doing so I reached in my pocket and pulled out a few folded notes. The gesture convinced him he was on to a likely winner, so he swiftly handed over the ticket. Thankfully it was the real deal. I stuffed the ticket in my pocket, handed him the money and waited. Then bang, he blew his top.

'Three thousand! I want 3000! Give me back my ticket!'

Not for the first time that day French arms began flying in all directions as the realisation of being short-changed hit home. Three thousand francs is more than £300 in English money, a piss-take for any football match as far as I was concerned. Usually I would never have the balls to front someone like this, but the argument with the Oxford lads must have fired me up to a new level, and with the game just 25 minutes away I had three short words for the tout: 'Fuck right off.'

Quickly he began to call his mates before turning to make a grab for me, but this time the English lads were prepared to back one of their own. As I stood by like an idiot, one lad brought me to my senses and told me to get myself off and inside while they crowded the tout and his mates. As I ducked down and made my way towards the police check point I received more than one pat on the back, taking off my top and placing my hat on my head as I went to make it hard for the tout's mates to track me.

Within seconds I was away from the crowds, past the police line and making my way up the semi-deserted street towards the ground. I honestly couldn't believe it. I couldn't believe I had had the bottle to pull it off. Some French muppet had thrown me a lifeline and I had managed to grab it with both hands without hesitation. As I bounced down the road I was shaking, half-expecting to see the tout and his mates come chasing after me, half-elated by the sight of the stadium in front. I was so pleased with myself for putting one over on that thieving French bastard that I couldn't help laughing out loud. During this tournament so many people had tried to rip me off; finally I had managed to get one in of my own. I had actually given him £100 for a ticket priced at £30, so in fact he had still come out well on top, but £100 was all I was prepared to pay following my earlier decision to fuck football off for good.

Of course, all those negative thoughts had now been kicked into touch. Football was the bollocks once more, my game, my buzz. Two minutes ago I hated everything and everyone, but now I was pumping again, alive with the rush that comes just before going into a major football stadium. Once again that familiar feeling suddenly flowed through my body. I checked the ticket once, twice, ten times. Amazingly I was about to see England play Argentina in the second round of the World Cup, a match that would have the eyes of the world focused upon it for so many reasons. All thoughts of being back home in the pub with my friends were gone. I felt like a kid in Willy Wonka's chocolate factory. I had the golden ticket. I was going to be one of the 35,000 who could honestly say, 'I was there.'

One more check of the ticket confirmed that I was in the end of the ground away from the main bulk of the English. With time running out fast I decided to try my luck and jump the queue for the English section. I was hoping that the sheer weight of numbers would force the hand of the steward at the ticket gate, but he was having none of it and directed me to the opposite end of the stadium, and in doing so jolted my mind with a rather nasty thought. The tout whom I had just ripped off appeared to have more than the one ticket when he approached me, and I suddenly realised that I could take my seat only to find him and a few friends eagerly awaiting my arrival.

As I jogged my way around to the correct turnstile I did my best to put such thoughts to the back of my mind, and while in the queue I had yet another stroke of luck after I began talking with the two English lads in front. It was obvious from their position in the stadium that they too had purchased their tickets via a tout, so I asked what sections they were in. As I had hoped, one of the lads found himself situated in the same section as me, so I offered to swap tickets with his friend. That way they could at least be within the same area, and I could avoid the risk of meeting old Froghead. Result. These two lads supported Stoke City, and they restored the faith I had lost in that club's supporters while up in Calais. I love Stoke now; go on City! As it turned out I also found myself with a much better seat, and one that should have been taken by someone working for the company Manpower!

The Stade Geoffroy Guichard is another perfect football arena, although quite why the French decided to play a second-phase match at such a small-capacity stadium leaves yet another question mark hanging over the organising committee. Unfortunately, these days little over 35,000 can squeeze into the stadium due to the introduction of new seated stands where there were once vast terraces that held 19,000 each. However, in their defence the nickname given to the stadium, 'The Cauldron', still rang true as the atmosphere reached boiling point.

As I took my seat I found myself surrounded by supporters from both countries. English supporters were beside and behind me, Argentinians in front. Potentially this was a disaster waiting to happen, an organisational nightmare that could come back to haunt Mr Platini and friends in years to come, but the reality was far different. Up here no one gave a toss. We all knew what was at stake, what the history was between us, and what by many areas of the press was expected from us. Instead of fighting we sang, acknowledging each other as football fans. All of us shared the desire to win, a love of our country and a love for football. Every one of us had struggled to get here for this moment, all just football fans living the same emotions.

Down at the front a vast section of Argies were doing their best to spur their team on, desperately trying to drown out the noise being made by the English up at the far end. Their chanting and the banging of drums were intense, but the sight of some fans prowling along the front and gesturing the action of cutting throats to England supporters was more than a little intimidating.

The teams arrive, lifting the noise to new levels. As expected, the national anthems of both countries receive little respect from the opposing supporters as recent conflicts return to the memory for five short minutes. Suddenly, the match is underway with the Argentinians settling down much quicker. Sitting next to me is Gary from Hull; a more focused man you could never hope to meet. His eyes do not look away from the pitch for a second. Every time England move the ball forward Gary grabs my arm. His actions are brought on by an intense mix of excitement and anticipation. At least I hope they were! As his fingers dig in he offers no apology, but then again here in the thick of it all I don't think he realises what he is doing. It is like having an unknown passenger on a train fall asleep next to you with his head coming to rest on your shoulder, slightly embarrassing but harmless.

Even with just a few minutes gone the Argentinians look a class above anything else England have faced so far in this tournament, then disaster. Seaman clatters down the Argie forward Simone to give the South Americans a penalty. The Argies around me jump to their feet, punching the air and hugging each other, while we sit still, cursing under our breath. Silence begins to fall, faces become hidden behind hands,

Gary's fingers dig in hard. Batistuta steps up; 1–0 Argentina. The stand I am in erupts like a volcano, a mass of pale blue and white. Down at the front the Argentinians climb the perimeter fence, shaking it backwards and forwards in frenzied celebration. At the far end I can see the movement of the English fans doing their best to lift our lads, but their chanting is completely drowned out.

Then the gaps start to appear. At the far end, where the English are positioned next to a large group of Argies, people start to move. The punches thrown are clear to see. For a few panic sets in. They do their best to escape, while the police remain motionless down at pitch side. The gap grows bigger as a few dozen England fans force some Argentinians from their seats and claim the ground they have taken as their own, arms out wide, wanting and waiting for more. There is no retaliation from the pale blue and white, though some refuse to be intimidated, refuse to move. Their team has just taken the lead, they want to celebrate. More English move forward, only this time they come to make the peace. They quickly outnumber the troublemakers and calm the lads looking for more by making a barrier between the two groups. From down at the pitch side the police turn to watch but remain unwilling to act.

Suddenly, attention is focused back on the pitch. The goal has shaken our lads, who are now beginning to come to life. Owen races clear, runs across the penalty area, knocks the ball past the keeper and tumbles. We appeal in hope rather than belief, but the referee has given it. A penalty! The Argies around us can't believe it. *He dived!* I can't help thinking that they are right, but we go mental.

Remember the Hand of God.

The passion reaches new levels. All ideals of gentlemanly play shot to pieces. Suddenly it's our turn to hold our heads.

Shearer steps up. He never misses, Shearer, but somehow I know he will this time. When it really matters. The Argies at the front do their best to put our hero off. The walk back. The turn, the run-up. That split-second silence, thud. Mayhem.

YESSSSSS! GO ON SHEARER! HAVE THAT, YOU ARGIE BASTARDS!

England are level. Red, white and blue everywhere. Like those around me I become lost in the ecstasy of the moment, all self-control rendered useless. The Argies around us offer only side glances towards the madmen jumping in all directions. Suddenly it is those around us who seem a little intimidated, although the mass down the front are quickly back supporting their team.

Now we are watching a different game. England are fantastic. Fast, skilful, confident. Every move continues to bring pressure from the clutching fingers of Gary's grip, then, following a pass from David Beckham, Owen begins a run. Past one. Then another. We rise from our seats. Owen cuts across the pitch. The Argentine keeper Roa leaves his goal line. We watch, bent at the knees, coiled springs waiting to explode. Owen in full flight is free, the keeper is committed, the ball is smacked across goal.

YESSSSSSSS! FUCKIN' YESSSSSSSSSS! YOU FUCKIN' BEAUTY! YESSSS!

My God! Have I ever experienced a goal like that before? So special, so beautiful, so important! I escape Gary's grip, leave my seat, run down the gangway and stand proud atop the concrete entrance, punching the air, screaming. I am lost, out of control, pure unadulterated orgasmic ecstasy. A steward comes to pull me down.

Suck my fart, you no hope. Get a fucking life. I've just seen one of the greatest goals in English football history, so you can fuck right off.

'The Cauldron' is living up to its billing. England fans throughout the stadium are going wild, the noise deafening, the atmosphere electric. Once more England pour forward. Owen continues his runs, scaring the Argies to death. Shearer plays his tricks. Sol Campbell controls all around him, as does Adams.

My God, this is it! This is the England team we have dreamed of. A team that is going to win the World Cup.

My body is shaking with excitement. All those years of waiting have come to an end. I never really thought it would happen, but there it is, out on that pitch before my very eyes. I can't help but think of home for a second. What must it be like in the pubs and clubs back home? All my friends. Those that I have stood on the terraces with through years of heartache. This is our day, proof that it is all worth while, that it isn't just a dream.

As the English sing, dance and congratulate each other, the Argies down at the front remain faithful. They too have belief. They know there is still plenty of time left in this game.

Many words have been written about the football supporters of the world – the Italians are passionate, the Greeks vocal, the Dutch . . . odd – but the support being given by the Argentinians to their side is something else altogether. It is visual, aggressive, passionate and loud. Very loud. They appear to truly believe they are as much a part of the team as any of the players. That support and the role they play never lets up, not for one second. I have seen the supporters of Italy, Greece and Holland in action, as well as those from many other nations, but the Argentinians display a support that lifts them far higher than any others I have experienced. Owen's goal somehow urges them on even more. They know their team is in trouble, but unlike an Italian army these Argies are never going to desert. The contest between the two sets of supporters is as exciting as that taking place on the pitch: the ecstatic joy of the English against the burning desire of the South Americans. Only by actually being there can you experience the emotion, feel the noise banging at your chest. Only when you're there can you sense the fear, the hope, the inevitable.

The pace of the match remains relentless. The feeling that England need that extra goal keeps digging at my mind. As each second ticks away England get closer, but with the missed chances mounting up (Scholes misses an absolute sitter) I can't help but fear the worst.

With the half-time whistle approaching Argentina con a free kick right on the edge of the England penalty area. Here it is, the inevitable returning to shatter the dream. The second the referee makes the decision we all know. All that hard work, all that effort. The free kick is clever, too clever for the English defence. Veron's short pass, Zanetti's short run, then bang. On the stroke of half-time the scores are level at 2–2. The Argentinians go wild, I kick the seat in front, Gary turns and curses the floor. Finally this roller-coaster game is brought to a temporary halt, giving the players and the fans some much-needed time in which to compose themselves.

As I rise to catch my breath the Argentinians sitting in front of me turn and puff out their cheeks. I shake my head. All those around me are acknowledging similar gestures. I can't remember ever seeing such an emotionally charged 45 minutes of football in my life, all of us united in the pleasure and pain we have just lived through.

During the interval I head back down beneath the stand to find both groups of supporters mixing, buzzing with the excitement of the occasion. There are no angry words, no threatening gestures, just strained faces, exaggerated conversations, respectful handshakes. I desperately want to ring my friends so that I can share the moment, but so too do another thousand or so who have beaten me to the pay phones.

As I return to my seat the optimism grows once again. England played beyond my wildest dreams during that first 45 minutes. Argentina were shaken, and my confidence is high. I know England can do it, I know it.

The return of the players soon kicks the crowd back into action. 'God Save the Queen', 'Rule Britannia' from the English; drumming, chanting, bouncing and shrill whistling from the Argentines. The noise level rises once more and the game gets underway. For a split second I turn my eyes to take in those around me, when suddenly the England fans jump to their feet spitting their fury. Quickly I turn. Gary's hand grabs at my shirt, lifting me with it. David Beckham is lying face down.

The Argentinian Simone is the target of the abuse. Then the stadium erupts. As the referee approaches, Beckham kicks out and Simone falls. Now the Argies around me rise, arms flying, voices screaming. The referee changes course, his gestures now calling the Englishman, not the South American. A flash of red. Beckham is being sent off. At first it fails to register. The Argentinians in the stadium go mad. Those in front hug each other, blow kisses skywards, scream with delight. I, like those around me, remain standing, unmoved, blank in our disbelief. Then the truth hits home. The referee has sent off Beckham. The dream is dead. The hope, the prize, taken from under our noses by a mixture of stupidity and trickery.

Please God, no. Please don't let this happen, not when we are this close. Please.

Gary hurls his abuse forward. The English behind me stare at the floor head in hands. I sink back down in my seat.

Why us? Why does everything always go against us? Why is it these Argie bastards always, always come out on top? I don't fucking get it! Fuck it! Fuck! Fuck!

One hundred miles an hour the thoughts race through my mind, never getting an answer. At that moment I want to leave the stadium. I want to leave so that I can take some of the dream with me rather than sit and wait for that inevitable killer goal to arrive.

The next 40 minutes are pure hell, every decision against us providing an outlet for my anger. Every Englishman around me feels the same – cheated. Cheated by one of the enemy and one of our own. The South Americans in front of us are now still, scared to move as every incident brings with it a venomous verbal onslaught from myself and Gary.

Somehow the Englishmen on the pitch hold out as the Argies stumble their way forward. Each and every one of our players is wearing the shirt with a passion that I have never seen before, each one a hero, never giving an inch. Somehow England still manage the odd move forward, the Argies looking dazed, confused. Ten minutes remain.

The cross into the box is firm: from nowhere Sol Campbell arrives. Power, determination, strength. The cross hangs as we rise from our seats. The header, the shaking of the net.

Campbell reels away with his team-mates, clawing at his shirt. Gary and I share a split-second stare at each other to confirm the moment.

He's fucking scored! YESSSSSSSSSSSSSSSSSS!

We hug each other. We hug those behind us. We scream at those in front and give the rest of the world the two-fingered salute.

England have won! England have fucking won! The world did its best to stop us, but we've won, you bastards!

Gary then freezes, his expression changed. Once again the anger spits from his mouth. I face the pitch to see the Argies attacking. I shout at those around me, searching out the answer, only to realise that the referee has disallowed the goal. No one, but no one, knows why.

For the next ten minutes all I can do is sit and stare. No words, no gestures. This match has drained me and I am left with almost nothing to give until eventually the whistle blows to signal the end of 90 minutes. That whistle brings relief. What those ten men have done for their country, the supporters and for each other is remarkable. The Argentinians look shattered. England have grabbed a moral victory.

This time, as the two sides take a much-needed break, I refuse to return the gestures the enemy offer my way. How can these Argies, so undeniably passionate in their support, back such blatant cheating? What is it in their make-up that makes such actions acceptable among men? Before I couldn't help but have respect for their support, now I despise them.

As extra time starts I shake hands with the England supporters around me, united in the pride we have for our lads. Again we belt out 'Rule Britannia', defiant, heads held high, English and proud. Somehow the ten men continue to push forward, the Argies foxed, worried. The atmosphere remains tense and the promise of penalties tugs at the brain. Surely we can't hold out.

At the far end the ball is once again swung into the penalty area. Shearer rises and the Argentinian defender Jose Chamot goes with him.

HANDBALL! HAND FUCKIN' BALL!

The England fans behind the goal mirror Shearer's reaction, but again the referee plays on.

It was handball, I know it was. Gary saw it too. It was fucking handball, you bastard!

Gary lets the world know, backed up with a kick at the seat in front. I could see it from 200 yards away, as could all those with me, but yet again the man that matters, referee Kim Nielsen, refuses. Never again will I trust a man with such a long neck. He looks like a swan. I fucking hate swans.

I pace, turning this way and that. I have given up on the game, a game that is now clearly ten men true against twelve unjust. All I want is the game to be fair, not to be cheated. It was handball. Why doesn't someone stop the game, walk on to the pitch and tell the referee he got it wrong? Each decision that goes against us kicks at my stomach. All I want is one taste of glory. What do we have to do in order to live out our greatest moment?

The seconds tick by, penalties draw closer, the crowd becomes quieter. Finally, the whistle blows. We've done it. Somehow we've survived. For 75 minutes those ten men have given the bravest display of any England team. The whistle brings a sense of pride that has me gloating over the Argies sitting in front. England have won the game. I swear they have proved to the world that they were the better side. Those ten heroic lions out there on the pitch have restored my faith in everything English, and for a while the nerves subside. Again I shake the hands of the English around me, only this time the gestures have a different feel. I can see in their eyes the same look I know I have in mine, all of us knowing England will lose. Again I want to leave the stadium – well, at least half of me does. If I could just take that feeling home with me I would die happy, but the other half has to stay, has to experience the final moments.

Again the gods favour the Argies as the referee beckons the players towards our end of the ground for the penalty shoot-out, allowing the Argentine fans down the front the opportunity to play yet another role. Seaman takes position, a hero. Berti scores; 1–0 Argentina. First up for England is Shearer. After the game of his life the top man cannot fail. The Argie fans at the front cat-call, whistle, wave their flags, do all they can to unnerve him. Bang; 1–1. His stance belittles them, silences their baying mob. Oh, to be Alan Shearer for that split second! Campos takes the long walk forward for Argentina. For Seaman it appears to be just another game as he moves between the posts, whacking his gloves together. Campos takes aim, Seaman saves.

YEAHHHHHHHHHHHH, SEAMAN! SEAMAN, YOU BEAUTY! YEAHHHHHHHHHHHH!

The jolt through the body is intense. The rush, that beautiful instantaneous rush of sheer uncontrollability, mentalness, pleasure, disbelief, belief. All English hands point in the direction of a nation's hero. Gary and I hug each other, sharing a golden moment. Suddenly the feelings inside have changed. Belief returns, along with unrelenting nerves. My body begins to shake, and I mutter to myself as I place my palms upon my cheeks: *My God, we can win, we can win.*

During the mayhem Paul Ince has moved forward. I can't help but close my eyes and pray for him. Ince fails to score. It is the turn of the Argentine fans to go wild while we remain still, blank again.

Veron is the next up. Seaman can do it. I am certain he will save it, as is Gary. We tug at each other's arms as Veron takes stride, expectation rising. The ball hits the back of the net; 2–1. There is no time to compose myself. The sight of Merson suddenly has my heart sinking. I can't help but feel for him as he makes the long, lonely walk. A great player, an exciting player, but a player whose career has taken so many twists and turns. All agree that Merson is destined to fail. I tell myself not to blame this man, a man who has suffered so much. He turns, shoots, scores. I thank God for The Merse.

Gallardo steps forward to challenge Seaman. He doesn't want to waste time; his spot-kick is cool. 3–2, and a jog back to the centre circle. Michael Owen comes next, 18 years old. What is going through his mind? The eyes of the world are upon him but he displays ultimate belief in his ability. This penalty kick could change his life. If he misses it could shatter him. He has everything to lose. Roa in the Argentine goal has no chance; 3–3.

From somewhere the atmosphere finds a new level. Now we are effectively down to sudden death as Ayala steps up to face the England number one. Desperately I try to regain some composure, try to look as if it doesn't matter. I find it hard to look straight ahead and view the goalmouth with a sideways glance. Ayala scores; I curse. The Argentine in front falls back down in his seat and appears to begin praying.

An English voice shatters my blank stare: 'Not Batty? Surely Batty's not taking one?' I look round to find him looking for support. His eyes fix on me. 'He's never taken a penalty in his life!'

The words register, but I don't want to hear them. I have no answer.

This time I turn to face the pitch. No sideways glare. If David Batty is brave enough, then so am I. The Argentine in front remains seated. Coward. Batty places the ball, Roa bounces from foot to foot. The English number eight turns, takes a few short steps, then turns again. Roa bends at the knee, waiting, ready to pounce. A split second later Batty shoots. Roa dives. England are out.

'I fucking knew Batty would miss that. I fucking knew it!'

I utter the words, but of course the truth is I knew nothing. Gary is gone, cursing as he flies past. Never shall we meet again. There is no goodbye. In front the seated Argentinian is buried beneath the bodies of his friends; on the pitch Batty is comforted by Roa. I turn to see those behind looking like the three wise monkeys, only sadder. One is seated, head in hands; the other two are standing, tears in the eyes of one while the other has his hands placed on the top of his head. In a calm voice, one says, 'Why Batty?'

'Why fucking England?' is all I can reply.

As I go to leave, my vision fixes on the Argentine in front.

Through all his delight I can't help but notice a little fear in his eyes. He shrugs his shoulders by way of consolation, and from somewhere I find it within myself to shake his hand and wish him luck. I don't mean it. Desperately I want to get away.

Outside I find my mind battling against itself to find the answers to so many questions. Here, English voices try to outdo each other, people wanting to air their opinion.

'Beckham, what was he doing?'

'Heroes ten, among them one fool.'

'Batty, why Batty?'

'The referee, the bastard referee.'

Floating above the constant conversation comes the jubilant singing of Argentinians still inside the stadium celebrating a famous victory. Their joy cuts hard as I battle against the crowd. Inside I feel numb, drained of all emotion, the game blanked from my mind. Then I find myself lost.

All I want is to get back to the coach, but no steward I ask has a clue as to what I am saying, so I find myself directed towards the main drag that heads to the town square. Among all these thousands of people I somehow manage to feel alone, then a hand grabs at my shoulder. Unbelievably, I turn to see Smurf. A rush of relief flows through my body, bringing with it some of the emotion brought on by the result. As we walk we talk about the match. Now I almost feel calm, relieved that the torture is over, pride at the display of our lads quickly banishing all disappointment. Smurf tells me that he managed to get a ticket for £200 just before kick-off, only to find himself situated in the same end as me but among the Argentinians down at the front, something that at times got a little scary.

Together we are told to board a bus that takes us to the main square; there we will find buses to take us to our coach park. We do as we are told, but this proves to be complete bollocks. We arrive at the main square to find no additional buses but plenty of local youths and dozens of riot vans. Suddenly the police jump into action. They board their vans and sirens start blasting my eardrums. Within seconds we find we are alone but for a few dozen dodgy-looking French lads. Quickly we turn and begin the long walk back towards where we have just come from. That threatening feeling most football fans come to know and hate begins pumping through my body, while I try my hardest not to look laddish or scared. Smurf and I walk the fastest hundred metres in history, both wanting to look back over our shoulders but at the same time not quite having the bottle to just in case we see something we don't like.

The realisation that time is no longer on our side has me beginning to panic. Neither of us has a clue how to get back to the coach park, and the thought of being left behind grows stronger by the second. At this stage I refuse to give up, so the pair of us break into a jog before a car pulls over and an English voice shouts at us. I recognise the guy driving from earlier in the day, and thankfully he offers to give us a lift back to the stadium as he is heading that way in order to pick up his mates. As we drive we pass a group of four Argentinians giving verbal to an English guy on his own. The driver slows the car and we watch before they move on, leaving him alone.

Our free taxi drops us off at the point where we were told to get the bus into town. I find the steward who wrongly directed us and give him a mouthful before we head back towards the stadium and the general direction of the coach park. Suddenly all the disappointment of England's defeat takes hold, and my head drops. Walking back past the empty stands we resign ourselves to our fate. On a crossroads up ahead is a small snack bar, and with hunger taking over we drag our heels towards sustenance. One last stab of hope has me asking a policeman if he knows the way back.

'Yes. That bus takes you there, but be quick, it's the last one.'

I can't believe my ears. Not only does he speak fluent English but he knows the way home. I love these French police.

Five minutes later the bus drops us at the coach park and I sprint away like Linford Christie on acid. The fields are as empty as when we arrived, all the other traffic gone, but over in the far corner I can see the lights of two coaches. With my last ounce of energy I force my legs forward, then suddenly there it is, like a pot of gold at the end of a rainbow. Boy, are they pissed off! While they line up to ask for explanations, give their opinion and generally get things off their chest, Smurf appears through the darkness like death warmed up, out of breath. The verbal falls upon deaf ears; I am sorry, but ecstatic at being saved. I love these blokes more than mere words can say; I love them for waiting, for not deserting us. Thank you, thank you, thank you.

The moaning quickly stops and we are on our way. On board are two additional lads who had found themselves deserted by their own coach party but had managed to cadge a lift, the pair of them as relieved as Smurf and I. As the events of the day replay themselves through my mind the disappointment grows weaker and tiredness takes over. All I want now is home, my wife, bed, England. Our lads didn't lose tonight, but sometimes the odds are stacked so high against you that you just can't win. It is time to leave St Etienne, leave France and leave the World Cup behind.

I have many opinions on David Beckham. Firstly he is an excellent footballer; secondly, he has a shit hair cut; thirdly, he is shagging the one I personally consider to be the fourth best-looking Spice Girl, Geri included, of course; and fourthly, I blame him for costing England a place in the quarter-finals of France '98, and therefore I shall hate him for ever.

My reason for hating David Beckham is based on the simple belief that, following his sending off, England just could not produce the same kind of attacking football that had the Argies shitting themselves for the first 45 minutes. At first the whole country shared that belief. In the days following England's exit from the tournament Beckham was billed as the most-hated man in England by the press and on the television news. His every move was followed, filmed and remarked upon as the anger of a nation fell firmly upon him.

Then the first cracks appeared as Ferguson began defending his star player. The press, never wanting to offend Alex and co. – sorry, PLC – soon joined in. They reminded us that it was

Ince and Batty that missed the penalties, not Beckham. But if Beckham hadn't acted like such a prick it might not have gone to penalties, a point slightly overlooked by the pundits, methinks! The press, so vehement in their attack on the player at first, now ran to that moral high ground they love so much, slagging Danny Kelly's Internet site Football 365 for offering the headline, 'It is our duty to haunt him'. Yet just days earlier one newspaper, so defensive now, dedicated a whole page to their 'David Beckham Dartboard', a cut-out-and-keep dartboard cover which had Mr Beckham as its bull's-eye.

Pleas to stop the hate came from every angle. Suddenly the villain was the England manager Glenn Hoddle, who found himself vilified for openly blaming the player for England's exit. Rubbish. All Hoddle did was tell it like it was. Beckham's sending off changed the game. Nobody, not even those with the most red-tinted glasses, can deny that. Hoddle never slaughtered the player, in fact he did quite the opposite. He stated that Beckham would play for England again, when many in this country wanted to hear different. He said that yes, the lad had made a mistake, but don't we all make mistakes at some stage? And most importantly, he stated that he didn't blame David Beckham for England's defeat. Hoddle could so easily have taken the stance of 'I told you so' following his dropping of Beckham from the earlier games, but despite the fact that the lad gave him the perfect excuse, he didn't. He stood by him. Let's get something straight here: I am not a Hoddle fan, no way. Any man who continually picks players such as Anderton and Sheringham can only be a cracker short of a cheese board, but he is not the villain of this little crime.

It doesn't matter what the press say, what moral high ground they take, David Beckham will never be allowed to forget what he did to this country. When he plays at Elland Road he will be hounded. When he goes to Upton Park, Anfield, or any ground in the country there will be hundreds ready to remind him. I hope every now and then it hurts, I hope it puts him off his game and I hope he feels the same pain that I felt when I saw Batty's penalty get saved with my own eyes. But I will leave Chris from Coventry to express his view on the boy we know as David Beckham:

> As long as I have a hole in my arse I will never forgive Beckham for what he did to the football supporters of this country. If he had been sent off for a full-blooded tackle we could have lived with it. If he had smacked an Argie into row ten in a fit of anger he would have been a national hero. Even if he had gone off crying, showing pride in the shirt of his country, he would have been forgiven, but he showed nothing. He strolled off the pitch, he never apologised properly to the fans, and he never showed the passion, the pain or the anger that the rest of the country felt. When Gascoigne got yellow-carded in Italy he showed he had what it takes. He cried at the thought of missing out on representing his country and became a national hero in a split second. I will never go and watch England again if that boy is picked for the squad, never. David Beckham doesn't represent me. He doesn't display the feelings I want to see when a player pulls on the white shirt of England. He deserves everything he gets in the way of verbals, and should never be allowed to forget.

Whatever Happened To 'The Great British Press'?

During France '98 the British media not only scraped the bottom of the barrel, but drilled through the wood and scratched the dirt underneath in the hope of producing the elusive shock headline they crave so much. The level of lazy, ill-informed, cheap journalism sunk further than the *Titanic* as they whipped up the frenzy one day only to claim the moral high ground the next. Articles so obviously written from behind a desk in London or Manchester rather than the streets and cafés of France filled not only column inches but the minds of Mr and Mrs 'I'll believe anything'.

The reporting of Marseille was desperate, a one-sided account for those back home that ignored the causes, the victims and, of course, the other side of the story. As they hunted out their soundbites and images in Toulouse, Lens and St Etienne, they chose not to report on the good behaviour but rather what they saw as a near-miss situation that could have gone off at any moment.

Reports on the hooligans convicted focused on the fact that some were married with kids and had the money to support them. My God, they didn't come from broken homes! Most had good jobs, even houses! One article even informed us the 'ringleader' James Shayler liked nothing more than three – yes, just three – pints of lager with a lemonade topping when out on the tiles.

In the *Guardian*, Robert Yates 'talked to hard-core hooligans about to set off for France'. Among them was Chris, 31, who comes from Portsmouth. He works in the City, is tall, articulate and well dressed. Chris is surprised that it all kicked off so quickly in Marseille. Really! And he is proud of the number of Category C hooligan telephone numbers he has stored on his mobile. With a combination of England, Tunisia and Marseille it was hardly a surprise. If 'Chris', with all his connections, was so taken aback then it's more likely he was a copper than a 'hard-core hooligan' in the know and I fear Yates was duped.

In the build-up to Lens we were told to expect World War Three. In the build-up to St Etienne it was the Falklands revisited, revenge for 'the Hand of God', and a riot waiting to happen now that the drink was back on tap again. But in reality it all went off kind of OK, didn't it! Not too much written about that. But some articles defied belief.

In one a journalist said he hooked up with a group of fascists known as 'The Front Line Boys'. The gang leader was a stocky thirty-something with the obligatory shaven head. There were stories of them climbing on top of vehicles, sending their boots crashing into the sides of cars and punching old men in the face. Inevitably, they are on the lookout for North Africans; and want to do the 'niggers', not the French or the Romanians. What surprised me most about this account was that the lads didn't mind this bloke they had never met before latching on to them, asking questions and observing their deeds without himself getting involved.

Articles such as these are a scandal. If they were a joke they might appear a little less offensive to the readership but they are offered as truth. I have never in all my days heard of a firm allowing a stranger into their world, a violent world where hangers-on just aren't tolerated. One article mentioned violence in the Place du Capitole, yet I was there on the night in question and saw that the square played host to vast impromptu football matches, not street riots. It was certainly surrounded by a heavy but respectful police presence, but it was definitely not a place that provided a hunting ground for fascist football hooligans out to do 'niggers'.

The articles cover every stereotype: the shaven heads, the lager drinking, the anti-IRA songs and the racist attacks. Fortunately, for those that live in the real world, it is the use of such stereotypical references that give the game away.

What Way Next For Football's Finest?

The Rupert Murdoch take-over bid for Manchester United (*plc*) was a master stroke, an act of pure genius. In one swift move Mr Murdoch proved that not only has 'the people's game' been lost for ever, but so too has the toy of the fat cats. Those that were once safe in their executive boxes are now waking up to the news that their pockets are no longer the deepest to be dipped into, and that they themselves are now open to a red-hot poker up the jacksy. But this move by Murdoch will not only have a major impact on domestic football worldwide, but could also herald the end of the World Cup competition as we know it.

At last some of those that have screwed the fans for so long are finding themselves being well and truly rammed, and as a fan who has found himself at the sharp end for far too long that is a pleasure to behold. Suddenly the world of football is on the verge of being turned upside down as a major competitor stakes his intention to grab all the cards and then deal them back out, but only to those who are willing to play by his rules. The media were caught on the hop, rocked by the move, instigated by one of their own. The remaining circus that has told us for so long that a winning Manchester United in Europe could only be good for the English game were shaken on to the defensive as they came round to the fact that their favourite topic of conversation was being snatched away from under their very noses. The soundbites came out in packs as the realisation that the rest could be forced to report on nothing but the leftovers hit home. 'What about football at grass-roots level?' The patronising, 'Long gone are the days when a football club represented the heart of the community.' And the biggest U-turn of all: 'This can only be bad for English football.'

The truth is we are not talking about English football any more. Through the advance in communications the world grows smaller each day. Mr Murdoch is a world player along with all the owners of this planet's top football clubs, so the inevitable has finally caught up with itself and the chosen few are to sprint off into the distance leaving the rest way, way behind. But while the media are busy ringing the bells of doom, I keep reminding myself of an old song often belted out by the great faithful at Elland Road. The tune has within it the words, 'Who the fuck are Man United?' This is a lyric that for many most certainly rings true, because for a vast number of spectators that actually dare to visit a football stadium on a Saturday afternoon, 'Man United PLC World' means little or nothing.

The assumption that all English football fans should care about MUFC winning in Europe is bullshit, and the thinking that we 'need' their greed down in the lower leagues is about as patronising as a Labour Party election promise. The terrestrial television companies still fail to grasp that many only watch in the hope of seeing the biggest team in the country get beaten by sides from great footballing nations such as Turkey. Mr Murdoch understands that, he understands that only too well, but then again his satellite company no longer needs to pander to such patronising commentary as he clearly views the bigger, worldwide picture.

Manchester United plc are a world marketing dream. BSkyB can beam their product live into the living rooms of Melbourne, San Francisco and Johannesburg as well as Nuneaton,

Ilford and Falmouth. MUFC are the biggest club on earth. United supporters' clubs throughout the world will be queuing up to buy the decoder and pay their subscriptions, and who can blame them as getting a ticket for Old Trafford is for most nothing more than a pipe dream. In the same way, you can't blame the shareholders for wanting to cash in on their invest-ment; after all, this is serious hard-cash generation we are talking about here. Big, big bucks. If you are going to sell the family silver, you can hardly get the hump when the new owners want to sell it on, can you? No, if you're looking for someone to blame then look no further than those that are now finding themselves on the end of the boot. The very people who sold the game to the sponsors in the first place, those top Johnnys at Lancaster Gate.

On the day when the top bods signed the deal allowing the first sponsor's name to appear on the front of a team shirt, football sold its soul to the Devil that is commercialism. Once the pound signs started flickering within those eyes, football was a goner, as suddenly everything had a price in the modern game. With the flood gates opened football quickly ran ahead of itself as the sponsors demanded maximum exposure for their investment. Even the names of the cup competitions were sold off, making the reading of some leading clubs' roll of honours almost laughable.

To the greedy that didn't matter; the bank account was growing fatter and growing fast. Pretty soon the ten per cent merchants began to sit up and take notice of football's rise to celebrity status. The agents moved in like leeches, demanding more by the day for their clients' services. Something had to give, or better still, someone. Slowly but surely, many fans began to find themselves being priced out of the game they had supported all their lives as loyalty became a dirty word. Concessions were scrapped, executive boxes built, and expen-sive seats replaced the faithful's terrace. As football worked hard to attract a new army of fans the old legions were unashamedly forced to sit at home and wait for the highlights on late-night television. For football's great leaders the blueprint was working, the new armchair fan providing yet another bargaining tool as the television companies fought like cat and dog to hang on to the wagging tail. The once-poor football club suddenly became a valuable commodity, and with this new-found popularity began turning themselves over to the world of businessmen and stockbrokers.

The traditional football club chairman, although desperate to hang on to a majority shareholding, slowly but surely found his arms being twisted. Big business demands that the man at the top acts in the best interests of all those who own a stake in the company, so very quickly many chairmen found the strings being pulled from every different direction. The invisible shareholders, not football people but money people, started to ask awkward questions regarding their investment, questions about the league set-up, the distribution of television money, and airing views on finding new ways in which to gain maximum returns from their business investment. Suggestions were tabled, motions put forward, and they brought with them the birth of the Premier League, the only place to be. This was the original football heaven, supposedly a place where the members looked after their own. But while most looked down their noses at those they had happily left behind, the top few were already wanting a bigger slice of the money bun. As greed got the better of everyone, leading to suggestions of breakaway after breakaway, surely someone must have realised that with football heading the way it was eventually there could only end up one or two winners. It was here that football had a last chance to take a long, hard look at itself. Unfortunately, it failed.

More money for television rights followed as Sky took a first finger hold, the first step on the way to securing the tight grip needed by the company so that it could begin to flex some serious muscle. Television money soon dictated that Saturday was no longer football day. The inconvenience to those that actually watched the game in the flesh wasn't an issue as every night became football night in the pubs, clubs and front rooms of the nation. By now the initial blueprint was beginning to cave in on itself. In selling football off so blatantly a new kind of supporter was created, one that rarely, if ever, attended a match but nevertheless demanded the product 'live' via the TV screen.

The same was happening the world over as the top clubs manoeuvred themselves into a position where they outgrew their respective domestic leagues and demanded to feature on a global stage. Big business at last had football firmly held by the balls, and the amount of money to be made will demand that the inevitable eventually comes to pass. FIFA's proposed plans to restructure the European cup competitions is little more than a delaying tactic, a last-gasp gesture to cling on to what was once their bread winner. With football now dictated to by the owners of television companies, multinationals, sponsors and advertisers, the game's governing bodies will eventually become powerless and there is absolutely nothing they can do to turn back the tide of money being waved under the noses of the elite.

So the big question is, where does that leave the rest of us when Man United and co. head off to battle it out to be crowned global kings? Well, if you believe the scaremongers, the journalists and the 'experts', domestic football is dead. Here in England it will never be the same again without the nation's top club, but then again their definition of domestic football differs from that of many football fans as it often stops short, at the bottom of the Premier League. For the rest of us, those down in the pit, the bottom three divisions and beyond, life is very unlikely to become that much different.

Personally, I want Man United to join the European Super League. I want them sprinting off into the distance to play Ajax and Barcelona, because as a supporter that follows a lower league club I honestly couldn't give a toss about any of that. To me that is all a million miles away. It's faceless, meaningless, remote and boring. Due to the present structuring and financial share-out policy designed by the league's top brass, my side will never be a member of the groovy gang, and over the last decade I have become accustomed to that little fact, so fuck 'em. I can live without the prospect of a trip to Old Trafford for a cup tie against United's reserves thank you very much, and I think you'll find that I am not alone.

My only feelings towards MUFC are feelings of sorrow for the true fans, those that actually once enjoyed a Saturday afternoon out watching their lads. I met many on my trip to France '98. They are as genuine as any, and have been shat on more than most. Now they are about to suffer in a way we will never understand, as even local rivalry is about to be taken away. No longer for them the Monday morning banter concerning Saturday's result against the teams supported by their work-mates. Who gives a toss if they draw with Paris Saint Germain or even Porto in a league no one bar them gives a chicken's ring about?

Make no mistake, when United shoot through, so too will much of the money currently being dished out among football's top dogs, and personally I don't think that is too bad a thing. As all cameras turn and point towards the European Super League, so too will the chequebooks. When that happens the lack of money then being invested back home in the top domestic division will very quickly take its toll. Many of our so-called top sides, those desperately hanging on in there for the last decade, could well find their worlds turned upside down, and their position in the league tables could well go with it. The best of the rest battling it out in the Premier League will soon find that the fat wage demands of their top foreign stars prove too much of a drain on the club's resources. For the rest of us, the financial gap between the top flight and the leftovers, forged by their greedy self-preservation demands, could soon begin to close and the smaller clubs could at last find themselves playing on a more even playing field.

For the clubs in the top flight these first few years of adjustment will prove hard. When the trend for following the big guns begins to fade, many of the new breeds will remove their replica shirts and tuck them away in a dark cupboard, only to be brought out again as an embarrassing reminder of their past, in much the same way as most thirty-somethings bring out photographs of themselves wearing high-waist trousers with side pockets and pie-crust shoes. At the top level the crowds will undoubtedly begin to fall as football loses its flavour. Like most things in life, football will one day find itself turning full circle, so in a desperate bid to win back the fans it so happily shafted, entrance prices will at last begin to fall. The problems faced by the top clubs will slowly but surely trickle down, but whereas a forced cut in the wage bill will affect the playing staff of the dream teams, those lower down the league will receive the good news with open arms.

Clubs such as Coventry, Southampton and Middlesbrough, presently living on the financial edge just in order to keep up, will find the going tough as their greedy star players, and more importantly those new-breed paying punters, desert in their thousands. Don't get me wrong, I know that City, the Saints and Boro all have a hard core of support second to none, but believe me, deserters there will be as every club has their percentage of hangers-on, so it follows that the bigger clubs have more than most. Don't be fooled, these clubs are being run on a gamble, a gamble that the rest, along with the hard core, will turn up week after week, but unfortunately their day at the races is coming to an end. Remember the dark old days at Ayresome Park? I never saw Boro pulling in 35,000 back then!

For the hard core the word 'support' means something. Through thick and more often thin, shoulder to shoulder. Living for the golden moments that wipe out the hours of suffering. Over the next few seasons many top football clubs will be on the verge of finding out just who their true supporters are. But for the Plymouths, the Burnleys and the Portsmouths, such huge percentage drops in attendance figures shouldn't materialise as these clubs have already learnt the hard lesson of living within their means, working their budgets around the hard-core support that will never desert them. For the faithful at clubs such as these, supporting their club isn't all about great football. Indeed, if that were the case, why is it that my club Watford, with the Gunners, Chelsea and Spurs all less than 20 miles away, can always rely on 7,000 turning up no matter what division they're playing in?

According to many, the upturn in football over the last ten to fifteen years has seen to it that the football supporter has never had it so good, but is that really the truth? It was easy to convince those who have never known any different, but for many older fans the glory days are but a distant memory. Standing in a group with your friends was much more of a buzz than the likelihood of having to sit next to someone you don't even know. Finding a place where you could sing without a care was better than having that slight feeling of embarrassment about what the person behind thinks of you. And yes, standing in the rain on a wet Tuesday was better, certainly better, than sitting down in the rain on a wet slab of plastic. If I sound like a boring old fart, then all I can say is that I must be. I know it's not everyone's cup of Bovril, but given the choice, and one day I hope that we might be, I know where my feet will be heading.

The same people stating those 'never had it so good' claims are also quick to impress upon us that the standard of football is now the best ever to have graced our playing fields, but here again I remain unconvinced. The influx of foreign players over the last decades is supported by the notion that they bring with them skills and experience that in the long term can only benefit the British game. Shite, I don't see the England team making huge strides forward. France '98 provided the proof of that. A defeat against Romania, then knocked out in the second phase by a side that found themselves rapidly booking taxis for the airport themselves isn't really that impressive, is it? And as for Scotland, well, one point says it all really. Many will state that the sponsors' hard cash has brought us a better game; all I see are higher wage demands. I do remember glory days, though; the days when English and Scottish teams ruled throughout Europe. We didn't have legions of foreign players in our top leagues then. Surely the best experience any young player can get is that of actually being out there learning his trade, not up in the stands watching some import. Only when that happens will English, Scottish and Welsh football develop and the home-grown talent we need begin to shine through.

When the money begins to drain, those foreign players, many of whom were here to grab that last big pay day, will head off back to mum. Those that go will have to be replaced, and in the process the domestic league tables could very quickly take on a whole new look as what money remains begins to change hands. Those that once relied on the fat chequebook rather than a strong youth policy will suddenly be forced to find their way again, and for many the going will be tough. Some, it would appear, have already given up the chase. The announcement in late September '98 by West Ham United that they were hoping to forge links with the Italian giants Juventus more than provided proof that the money was finally beginning to dry up at the top end of the market. By 'forging links', West Ham United seemed to me effectively to be saying they would give Juve's fringe players a run out if the Italians didn't charge them a fee. Who would have believed it, eh? The Hammers, Juve's reserves! From the money man's point of view a sound proposition, but for the paying supporters? Just how out of touch can they get with the people paying for their Armani suits? Unsurprisingly, the news didn't go down too well in Pie and Mash Land, and within a day of the original story breaking the east London club began issuing press statements denying any future speculation.

Football club directors continually fail to grasp the fact that we football supporters are far and away the strangest breed to walk this earth. If the dream is alive, then we want to live it. Give us something to cling to along with the opportunity of playing our part, and we'll be there. Football supporters will do all they can to help anyone acting in the best interests of their club. Life down in the basement can often provide the answers as to how true fans react when their club is being run by people that really care. Clubs such as Aldershot Town. Remember them? The Shots went bust, dropped from the league and apparently disappeared never to be seen again, a club branded as an inevitable casualty of football's brave new business world. Slowly but surely, and with the support of those who never gave up Aldershot have managed to work their way back up the football pyramid. This once sunken ship has been raised to find itself playing in front of bigger crowds than when it held league status, 2,000-plus being an average home gate for a fixture way down in the Rymans League. Rushden & Diamonds FC of the Conference are another example of a club that thrives on the heart of the community it represents. The vision of a chairman devoted to the club has been backed up by supporters in their thousands, with attendance figures and a stadium that are the envy of many Nationwide Division teams.

And then there is the latest victim of football's greed, Doncaster Rovers. In the season Rovers dropped out of Division Three, many of those running our game preferred to concentrate their attention on packing for France rather than heading north in order to help one of their own. During that relegation season a club that required less money to save itself than the average Premier League club pays out on their weekly wage bill was left to fend for itself, the supporters shat on, the players unpaid. With the hole waiting to swallow them up growing deeper each and every day, the football hierarchy once again did little to help. Once the receivers moved in and the last rat jumped ship, the club dropped like a stone before eventually being picked up by the hands of people who really cared, the hands of supporters who then took it back to the community it was originally set up to represent.

Only when this happens, and a club rediscovers its heart, can it truly begin to rebuild itself, a lesson some of the big boys are about to learn themselves, having to take night classes just to catch up. If a football club has heart then it has a chance. How else can you explain that while in Division Three Rovers struggled to attract crowds of a thousand-plus to Belle Vue, yet their opening games in the Conference were watched by an average of 3,500! Football fans – strange breed.

The supporters and current boards of football clubs such as Bournemouth and Charlton Athletic have proved to those in control just how it should be done. Like Aldershot, Charlton very nearly lost their league status, but thankfully this particular south London outfit managed to hold it together, but only just. Charlton were lucky; they still had a few true fans on the board rather than shareholders. They had some directors who, when it came down to it, cared more about the club than the profits, and once the greedy were weeded out the fans backed them in a way that has never been seen before. Working together they harnessed enough collective power to enable them to force the once hostile local council into action and provide them with a home. Collective fan power proved to the council officials that a thriving football club, one that lives, breathes, works and represents the community in which it is based, is worth more than its weight in gold. It brings the people together, it instils pride and it places the area on the map like no multi-complex or business park could ever do.

Charlton now have in place a board of dedicated supporters that runs a club whose aim it is to represent and serve the community in which it is situated. When the shit hit the fan, like all others this club was left to die a slow death. As football consoled itself in the belief that some clubs were bound to fold, the supporters of Charlton refused to hang up their banners. Through perseverance and belief they have proved to the world that passion and business can live hand in hand. Yes, a football club has to be run effectively and efficiently, but not above all else; there comes a point where business needs to take a back seat. Not everything has a price and not everyone can be bought. Charlton provide an example to us all. I, for one, hope that they, more than any other club (bar my own, of course), have managed to work their way into such a position that they could well find themselves on the brink of being one of this country's finest.

It was sickening to see and hear the way the media portrayed the Londoners' arrival in the top flight. The very same media people who now find themselves on the defensive were oh so patronising towards cuddly little Charlton. Here for a season, then back to the neverland. That self-proclaimed voice of the fans David Mellor loved to remind any listening audience that he launched 'his' Football Task Force at the Valley. The truth of the matter, of course, being that his road-show only rolled up once the hard work had been completed.

BSkyB's announcement that they were bidding for United was the first major signal that the meal ticket is about to be taken away from the majority of the greedy, and I for one will not be sorry. The sooner the money men in the City begin to steer their cash away from football the better. It is only when that day arrives that the gap so enthusiastically forged between them and us, rich and poor, will begin to close. Greed has chewed away at football for far too long, but at last the self-selected few from the past decade are about to get a good hard dose of their own medicine.

It has never been good for English football to have teams pull players from the national team under the disguise of injury, sickness or personal trauma. It's not good for English youngsters to be overlooked because the chequebook prefers to stretch across continents in search of the next best thing. And it has never been good for the fans to have players, managers and directors alienate, lie to and cheat them.

Inevitably the day will soon come when English football runs well and truly up its own arse. The bubble will burst for all but one or two of the greedy bastards that have taken the sport for all they can get, while the rest were left to pick up the pieces. Hopefully the money men will then turn their attention to building multi-screen cinemas, shopping malls and leisure complexes, and we the fans can have our game back at the 'grass-roots level' that has suddenly become so popular to talk about.

But I have one last word of warning. The European Super League will never prove to be the golden egg for football's big guns. Once this brave new world has been exposed as not being the major spectator attraction it was supposed to be, the men pulling the strings will move on to look for the next big thing. Suddenly Man Utd v. Kiev and Bayern Munich v. Porto won't seem quite so attractive as England v. Brazil or Argentina v.

Holland. Now that is a thought: a World National League. The people at the top have already aired their views on the 'lesser nations' taking too many qualifying places at France '98. Through their reorganisation of the European cups they have already displayed their desire to look out for the top footballing nations' best clubs, so why not do the same for the world's greatest competition?

A World National League, a league with two or three divisions, with signed players, managers and boards of directors, will one day become the brainchild of one or another big, big player. But unlike the European Super League, this one might just work. Supporters would for once be united, just as they are now behind their nation's finest, and at the same time domestic football could well find itself left alone, untouched and playing the role it was originally set up to play – that of representing the community in which the club finds itself situated. And who knows, we might even let Man United back in so that they can join the party too!

This whole issue regarding the role of the media's involvement in buying football clubs turned out to be important for me in a way I could never have foretold.

Throughout my trip to France '98 I carried with me a small hand-held camcorder with which I intended to film research that would be used to write this book. As you have read, the events that unfolded before me provided a life experience I shall never forget, and the footage I recorded captured most of those moments in a way I could never have dreamed of.

Once I had returned home for good I showed the video to a contact of mine who couldn't believe what she was seeing. She sat back in horror at the scenes I had recorded in Marseille, both on the opening night and down on the beach where the riot well and truly kicked off. The woman in question felt the evidence I had gathered throughout my trip was an honest portrayal of what it was really like for me and thousands of others, and was so shocked by what I had filmed that she immediately set me up a meeting with Carlton Home

Entertainment with a view to making a video release. Thankfully for me Carlton agreed, so on Monday, 14 September 1998 *Teargas and Tantrums* the video was released on an unsuspecting British public.

Now I always knew that through this video I would be lining myself up for yet more criticism. Throughout my writing career my shoulders have had to become a little stronger with each publication as the press and the football-related media once again roll out their stereotypical clichés. Unfortunately, you soon learn in this business that the second you stick your neck up out of the trench the bullets start flying, and if you have been honest and admitted to having a slightly dubious past then the bullets quickly turn into rockets.

Through the previous books I have co-written for this publisher I have openly admitted that I was once involved in football violence. I have gone on to explain how and why I became involved and ultimately what it was that made me stop. All this was done in the vain hope that a better understanding of the problem would in some way help the people trying to solve it, but the point I have tried to make appears continually to have been ignored by those that supposedly know better.

The last few days before the release of the video were spent ringing friends, relatives and the new in-laws warning them of what they might be reading about me over the next few days, but as I sat back and waited for the inevitable to happen I had overlooked one key factor that both Carlton and myself could never have prepared ourselves for. The news that Rupert Murdoch had put in a bid to buy Manchester United through his television company BSkyB had hit football, sending shock waves to the grass roots and pound signs to the shareholding boys in the City. Suddenly events on the pitch became secondary as all the top clubs opened talks with television companies through fear of being left behind and in the hope of hanging on to United's coat tails. Personally, I couldn't give a monkey's tit about Manchester United, but the problem I had was that their biggest rivals and Premier League champions, Arsenal, had now become the target for Carlton Television, the parent company of Carlton Home Entertainment. Was it coincidence that some of the strongest criticism of the video, and of the company behind it, came from the Murdoch press? They argued that Carlton had showed themselves unfit to own a football club, and I was suddenly caught up in a battle between the media giants.

I am proud to say that I am not part of the football world inhabited by the likes of Murdoch and Mellor. I don't have to say the right things or play the media game. If I want to slag someone, I don't have to consider if it will prevent me from being invited to the executive box. If I want to allow true fans the opportunity to air their point of view, I will, and have done so via this and all my previous books. I do not agree with all of what I get sent or told, but if it is valid, honest and true, who am I to censor it? And that is where we come to the crux of this whole business. There was a stage during all this that I honestly felt Carlton would pull the video from the shelf in the hope of steering criticism away from their organisation. Let's face it, at the time the asking price for Arsenal was somewhere in the region of £200 million, and in the great scheme of things that made this video look about as big as a gnat's nipple. The questions I was asked relating to Carlton's involvement by various reporters have me firmly believing that some form of strong-arm tactics bordering on censorship were being brought to bear on that organisation. Thankfully, Carlton held strong.

I will point out here on their behalf that the views expressed in that video are mine and mine alone, and I strongly stand by them. Carlton simply saw the footage I shot as a valid documentary of the events one man witnessed during his trip to France, and you can't really argue with that. The film of the beach riot and that taken during the opening night is there for all to see uncut, unlike much of the news footage that was shown back home at the time. What makes the film sent back by the reporters working for BSkyB, the BBC or any other organisation different from mine? The producers of their news programmes know the money shots and their shows were full of them. The running battles, bottle throwing, bleeding heads – the news programmes had it all. I could see what was going on and I could tell how it was going to be reported by the great British media after my very first night, which funnily enough ended with a drink in the company of a reporter from the *Sun* newspaper.

Having a camera in your hand can often prove dangerous, and there were numerous times when I was threatened with a good hiding if I failed to switch the thing off (come to think of it, that's how I first encountered Wiltshire). Despite the threats I stuck at it, because I felt there was a story to be told that no one else was going to tell. I can live with the press slagging me off – this wasn't the first time, and I'll make sure it won't be the last either – but if my work makes one person sit up and take notice then it is worth the hassle. I can't narrate lies over film that clearly shows what happened. Carlton understood that, and I think in doing so showed that they are more in touch with the realities of what fans often have to suffer than any of the other media companies desperately trying to get their hands on a football club and sell it as a worldwide media event.

Is That It Then?

Let's face it, when Batty had his penalty saved the World Cup was to all intents and purposes over. OK, so there were some nice little moments – Croatia stuffing the sausage eaters 3–0 was one of them, although not everyone would agree. That scoreline resulted in two people losing their lives: a Croat woman accidentally shot dead during over-exuberant celebrations back in the homeland, and Englishman Ronny Redhead, beaten to death at a German village beer festival following the Germans' woeful display.

Back in France, Dennis Bergkamp scored the best goal of the tournament to send the Argies packing, while the only good thing to come out of France reaching the final was that some of those greedy bastards suddenly found themselves having to pay over the odds just to see a game of football. Nice one, God. And all right, you had to watch the final. I did that round my friend Tom's house in Golders Green, and my memory of France v. Brazil? Shit game, great piss-up, but in reality, who gave a toss? All in all, the football at France '98 was piss-poor, the skill level average at best, and the entertainment rating struggling to reach 4 out of 10.

As for the England team, well, if you're going to get knocked out you may as well go out in style. Faith in English football was restored by the performances in Lens and St Etienne, and in many ways the team did the next best thing to actually winning the bloody thing. Surely no one can deny that England v. Argentina was the outstanding game of the tournament, with, for me anyway, USA v. Iran running in second. Obviously I am not putting that down to the skill level, more to the sheer passion generated by the crowd.

Once England were out and I found myself safely back home, it all seemed so far away, uninteresting, a mere stopgap until the new season got underway. It was good to see the corporate sponsors get their arses kicked. Adidas had red cards galore along with the most wanted man since Fred West in their ranks, namely Mr David Beckham. Nike also saw red and had the added scandal surrounding their dream team, Brazil, in particular the inclusion of Ronaldo in the final! Commercialisation, a wonderful thing!

The passion that France '98 generated around the world was quite simply mind-blowing. Rioting on the streets of Marseille, the student halls of Kenya, even outside pubs in sleepy old Hertfordshire. The number of deaths, suicides and hospitalisations, all brought about by 22 men kicking shit out of a small white ball, is hard to place a figure on, but it is definitely more than you get during your average Wimbledon tennis week. The importance we place on football is unbelievable, especially at a time when the people of Sudan were dying of starvation.

Personally, I learnt many lessons during France '98. I should have realised in advance that a game so willing to screw its lifeblood at club level would turn the screw even further when the big stuff was on offer, but not even I was prepared for the depths they would sink to. But that said, the faith I had in my fellow followers of football manifested itself tenfold as we came together in search of those special memories. Englishmen, South Africans and Argentines all chasing that same dream, and for the most part chasing it side by side and showing respect for each other as we went.

I found to my delight that when abroad with England you are never alone. It was OK to be proud of your origins, and better still no one told me I was wrong to act in such a manner, just as they never told off the Chileans, the Scottish or whoever for behaving in exactly the same manner. All that crap was left to the media back home, a media machine quick to whip it up but even quicker to knock it down. I learnt that the only way to find the truth is to go out and experience it for yourself. Go live it, breathe it, feel it.

And will I ever do it all again? Too fucking right I will. Despite the hassle, the danger and the greed, I wouldn't have missed being among those supporters for the world. Although I doubt very much I'd try quite so hard to see the actual matches! And you try organising that one, FIFA!

But the greatest lesson I brought back from France was this. As football continues to change itself and its fan base, repackaging, redesigning and relabelling itself, I too as a football supporter have finally begun to change. The money-grabbing shambles that was France '98 brought me to this conclusion: slowly but surely I have become less of a fan of football, and more a fan of football supporters. And you know what? I don't feel quite so alienated any more.

Keep the faith.